# THE
## CASE
### FOR THE

# WORKING MOTHER

Dorothy Whyte Cotton

STEIN AND DAY / PUBLISHERS / NEW YORK

*For* JOHN *and the children:*
MIKE,
MARY,
JOHNNY, *and*
MUFFY.

# CONTENTS

## NOT A "MOTHER-SUBSTITUTE," BUT A MOTHER-HELPER

## AT HOME AWAY FROM HOME

## THE DROP-OUT PROBLEM

# FOREWORD

MANY mothers have no choice at all about whether to take a job outside the home. They may be separated from their husbands, or they may be widows or divorcees who need to earn money to provide adequately for themselves and their children. Or they may be women whose husbands are ill, or poorly paid, or unemployed. While these mothers deserve consideration and attention, they are not the primary concern of this book.

Nor is the book addressed to those thousands upon thousands of stay-at-home mothers whose many activities stimulate their minds and satisfactorily fill their days. It is not our purpose to goad them into a

11

frantic perusal of the Help Wanted ads. Shaming mothers into abandoning a life they like for a job that might "fulfill" them as individuals has recently become a popular, if dubious, pastime.

Why then *The Case for the Working Mother?* Based on hundreds of interviews, it is intended for those women who have chosen to work, as well as for the many others who are in the process of determining whether an outside job is both possible and right for them. For many modern mothers, the need to be employed outside the home—as well as in it—is as real and pressing as one born solely of urgent economic necessity. Countless woman are proving that motherhood can be successfully combined with an outside job, not only with no detriment to their families but, quite to the contrary, with many positive benefits.

In this book you will find guidelines (there are no rigid rules) to help you determine what is likely to work best for you and your family. The book examines some of the reasons mothers choose to work, and the effects on their children. It takes up the question of mother-helpers, discusses schools and their role. It looks at the ways some mothers handle their dual responsibilities, and offers practical management tips. It has something to say about the education of women and job opportunities for them. And it touches on society's need to come to grips with the "quiet revolution" in mothers' employment outside the home.

In short, if you have an outside job or think you

want one, this book will attempt to make things easier for you by citing the combined experiences of many mothers who derive concrete rewards from working. Their discoveries can help you avoid the pitfalls inherent in a double career.

# 1

## THE FALSE FACES
## OF FEMININITY

PRACTICALLY everybody has something to say about the American mother. There is fairly general agreement that her like has not been seen before in any other culture, any other place. She is harangued, adored, envied, ridiculed. If she works outside the home, she may be described as either a Superwoman or an Emasculator. If she is content to stay at home, she can expect to be labeled a Ministering Angel—or a Victim. Praised or berated, she is the subject of endless debate: what is her "place"; what are her needs; how can they be met?

One has only to pick up a daily paper, a slick magazine, or a learned journal to discover how lively the controversy is. But much of the discussion bogs down in invective, which serves mainly to heighten the confusion and compound the dilemma. Because the role of women so intimately affects the nature of a society, many deeply personal feelings and attitudes are involved or threatened. The whole issue of woman's place is charged with emotion.

## MOTHER, GO HOME

The working mother—the special concern of this book —commands her share of detractors and boosters, with the former far outnumbering the latter. Yet over the mounting decibel level of criticism one can hear the sound of more than 8,000,000 pairs of heels clicking off to work. This large-scale movement out of the house and into paid employment began in World War II, when manpower shortages made the recruitment of women a "must." The movement is obviously showing no sign of reversing itself. At this moment in our history, one out of every three mothers with children under eighteen has a paid job, either full-time or part-time. This is the highest figure ever reached in the United States, and Labor Department statisticians predict that it will hit the ten million mark during the decade ahead.

This revolution in women's employment has disturbed many people. While our society no longer frowns on *women* who work outside the home it is

not totally prepared to smile on *mothers* who do. Only
in times of emergency has any whole-hearted encouragement been given to the working mother. During
wartime she was hailed as the darling of industry.
Such approval, however, did not last long. Soon after
the crisis passed, working mothers were urged to exchange their dungarees for dishwashers, their test
tubes for mixing bowls; and when they did not, they
fell from grace. Even today, in an era of increasingly
rapid and widespread social change, many outmoded,
if not outworn, attitudes persist.

Because the working mother alters the traditional
—i.e. comfortable—image of motherhood, she still is
not altogether socially acceptable in some quarters.
The question goes: How can a woman be a good and
successful mother and also work outside her home?
The viewers-with-alarm regard the working mother as
an upsetting phenomenon—a distortion of the familiar—different somehow from her stay-at-home con-
temporaries, perhaps dangerously threatening. These
are all familiar reactions to change. And it is understandable that many people wonder about, and feel
vaguely disturbed by, the quietly revolutionary developments that are drawing millions of mothers into
the labor force. While not demanding a return to
the "good old days," even were that possible, many
critics are not yet prepared to accept the new facts
of life. Old prejudices die slowly, even in the face of
new realities.

## A GAME ANY NUMBER CAN PLAY

A good many of the important changes in the lives of American women have been noted so frequently in the press and elsewhere that a bright ten-year-old could probably recite most of the items on the list: the earlier marriage age, the longer life span, the free time that mechanized homes and outside services make possible, the increasing equalitarianism in the relations between the sexes.

But despite these now familiar actualities that call for new ways of thinking and acting, the old clichés continue to be bruited about. Some askance-lookers find it less taxing to dredge up an ancient saw than to formulate a new opinion or modify an anachronistic attitude. While the most die-hard critic today might find it foolish or embarrassing to assert unequivocally that "woman's place is in the home," many voices can be heard proclaiming that "motherhood is a full-time career"—any less devotion to *kinder* is guaranteed to start Junior down the road to ruin.

But who can take seriously this notion of motherhood as a *full-time* career for every mother? Latest figures reveal that the average mother today has had her last child by the time she is twenty-six. That makes her only thirty-two when her youngest child is ready for first grade. No one would deny that her school-age children still need her very much, but do they really need her full-time? Devoting herself exclusively to a child, being completely wrapped up in his every move, may well stultify his development. The unwholesomeness of overprotection has been well documented. The really successful mother helps her youngsters to become independent by knowing how to snip the apron strings at appropriate ages and stages. If motherhood is a full-time career, it is the only one on record which demands that a person become dispensable in order to be successful.

If the full-time career bit does not fit some of today's mothers, there remains a host of handy calumnies waiting to be tried on for size. The working mother has been denounced as overaggressive. She has been accused of de-sexing her husband. Berated for unconsciously rejecting her children. Charged with causing juvenile delinquency. And branded as totally unfeminine. Why all this intemperate name-calling? The noisy pastime of substituting labels for thought has never illumined anything. We all know stay-at-home mothers who "martyr" themselves for their families—to no one's good, including their own. Or others who browbeat their husbands. Or some who neglect their children. Or still others who spend their days in assorted bars or beds.

Trading epithet for epithet is a game any number can play, but it is neither helpful nor intelligent. More than that, it is clearly destructive, serving only to blur the issues and obscure the real questions. The answers are far from simple; but if we are ever to find them, we will do better to examine the situation in all its complexity than to hide behind angry words.


## NO MAGIC FORMULA

Being an effective mother (working or not), rearing happy, healthy, responsible children, building a successful marriage—these have always been the most subtle and difficult of all human endeavors. Even Pollyanna could not pretend that the human race has yet come up with all the answers.

Those mothers who devote themselves exclusively to the care of their families can chalk up as many difficulties with their youngsters as those who do not, and working mothers have their own·built-in set of unique problems with their families. No two working mothers are alike. No two stay-at-home mothers are alike. There is simply no "always right" solution to be discovered in any one special prescription for parenthood. Just as staying home will not automatically make a mother "good," neither will going to work automatically make her "bad." One thing is certain: no clear-cut pattern of what a mother should do, or be, exists to fit *all* mothers.


## THE "EITHER-OR" CONCEPT

The concept of the "whole" child has gained universal acceptance in our culture. As far back as 1930 the

White House Conference on Children made a plea to all who contribute to the welfare of children—parents, teachers, physicians, clergymen—to consider each child as a total individual.

It was recognized then that for any valid appraisal of a child, one aspect of his life could not be investigated to the exclusion of others. It has become a pediatric and pedagogical truism that the child must be viewed as a whole, not in segments. This perfectly reasonable concept has permeated the popular as well as the professional literature on child care and development. But one rarely finds it extended to a consideration of mothers. It would seem equally obvious that to be a "whole" mother one must be a "whole" woman, first of all. Yet the notion is still prevalent in our society that a mother is somehow unnatural if she wants to combine the responsibilities of a home and children with an outside job. Is it any wonder that many a working mother finds herself asking such questions as: Am I really doing right by my family? Am I neglecting my children? Short-changing my husband?

Society plays a dirty trick on women when it forces them to plague themselves with questions such as these. It is not a matter of *either* home *or* work. "The conflict between job and children," according to Dr. John Levy, the late Associate Professor of Clinical Psychiatry at Columbia University's College of Physicians and Surgeons, "is not nearly so important as the conflict between what society says mothers should be and what they are." It is nonsense to assert that a mother who works prefers her outside activities to her children. Levy deplored the fact that:

> so much destructive feeling should have been built up on society's part around the supposed dangers of neglecting our children. Not only is a good deal of achievement lost to the world in general by parents' inabilities to enjoy their own accomplishments and ambitions because of fear of neglecting the children, but the family is no better off for this self-denial. If parents are made to feel that they are not devoting enough time to their homes, they feel guilty. If they give up some of their own interests to give more time to the children, they feel resentful about the high price paid for parenthood. Between guilt and resentment as constructive emotions there is very little to choose. When we feel guilty we punish ourselves, when we feel resentful we punish the other fellow. In the end both solutions get nowhere . . .

The *either-or* concept, which is both unreasonable and unfair, has contributed to this impasse. The "whole" mother does not work as an alternative to having her home and children. She knows perfectly well that there is no comparison between the satisfactions of even the most exciting work and the continuing rewards her own children give her. She knows how much motherhood enriches her life, but she is aware, too, that it is far from the final chapter. While she values her role in the family far above her work role, she does not automatically resign from all other adult interests and pursuits when she becomes a mother. For her own sake, as well as for her husband and children, her activities must extend beyond her own backyard and outside the comfortable closeness of her immediate family. If she limits her horizons to the kitchen and the nursery, what can she contribute to the intellectual development of her children? How can she help them grow in taste and in values if she herself does not grow?

## THE "MYSTIQUE" MISTAKE

In extreme support of the view that a woman should give herself the chance to get out into the larger world, there is a new conviction currently fashionable in lamenting the parlous state of womanhood. The argument in some quarters is that in the last two decades, women have been forced to emphasize their femininity at the expense of their humanity. They are thought to have been coerced by advertising (and correlatively by TV and the women's magazines) into feeling that the end-all of their being is in wall-to-wall Wifedom and Motherhood. They have supposedly been brainwashed into thinking that they are truly "feminine" only if they can be enraptured by a new detergent and fulfilled by the creativity of adding an egg to the cake mix. This syndrome has been identified and labeled the "Feminine Mystique."

But ridiculing stay-at-home mothers as gullible fools hoodwinked by Big Bad Advertiser is as pernicious as shaming other mothers out of working by branding them Neurotic Malcontents. There is not the slightest doubt that advertising does present a false face of femininity. But while advertising obviously has the power to whet consumer appetite—what else is its function?—it is powerless to enslave the American mother in her own home. Madison Avenue did not invent marriage, or children, or homemaking. It is certainly questionable that mothers who stay home do so mainly because they have been "sold" a bill of goods, that they are victims of, shall we call it, a Feminine Mistake. To underestimate our culture's need for women who desire simply to be intelligent and perceptive wives, mothers, and citizens is, to put it in the kindest terms, dangerously shortsighted.

More and more mothers who make it evident that they want families *first* are making it equally evident that they want something else besides. For a very large number that something else includes such important volunteer activities as working for improved schools, better libraries, needed hospitals. Volunteer mothers teach in nursery schools, serve on mental health committees, work in cancer-detection clinics. The list of significant contributions many of

these mothers make not only to their own development but also to the welfare of their communities—
and hence to the welfare of their own families—is
endless.

## NO BED OF NEUROSES

The notion that only neurotic women want paid jobs
outside their homes needs to be laid to rest. A quick
look around at one's friends, neighbors and relatives
reveals that neither the home nor the office has any
monopoly on neuroses. In the old days, when working
outside the home was indeed uncommon, it must
have demanded a motivation of iron. Those who
chose to work in the face of nearly total disapproval
may well have been power-drive types. But at a
time when employment of mothers is widespread, to
level such a charge against a whole group is patently
absurd. Dr. Mirra Komarovsky, the eminent sociolo-
gist, has pointed out:

> Today women pursue professions for the same
> mixture of vanity, curiosity, desire for service or
> for prestige, instinct of workmanship, and so on,
> which in addition to economic drives also moti-
> vate men.

Not to be taken seriously, either, is the new
snobbism which concerns itself only with the "creative" mother—the artist, the writer, the scientist, the

actress. Encourage her to use her talents, the current nonsense runs, but let the "untalented" ones flounder as they will. Of course, creative women deserve all the encouragement they can be given, but what about all the other mothers who want to go out to work? Have they no contributions to make; are their needs not to be taken seriously? Patterns for self-realization and growth take many forms. The trained bookkeeper who is bored with keeping just household accounts, the secretary whose unused skills are getting rusty, the technician who yearns to get back to the lab—all of them deserve their chances for fulfillment. A condescending or derisive attitude toward any group of mothers cannot but be a disservice to all mothers, indeed to our whole society. If all working mothers today were to quit tomorrow, the entire economy of our country would suffer a severe shock.

### WHAT'S IT WORTH?

For the sizable numbers of mothers who have chosen to work, their decision more often than not serves to enrich, rather than impoverish, family life. Countless working mothers and their families can attest to the fact that there are intangibles as well as tangibles to be gained. Obviously, many of the 8,000,000 mothers at work are forced to earn because they are the chief support of themselves and their children. Yet the

Bureau of Labor Statistics reports that the major increase in the last several years in the proportion of
mothers working has been among those living with
their husbands and among those above the lower income levels. In other words, the highest rise has oc-
curred among those who were not *forced* to work.
As Mrs. Katherine B. Oettinger, Chief of the Children's Bureau, puts it:

> The mother who works to help buy a home, to
> insure a college education for her children, to
> make possible a real vacation . . . or to help
> get the new TV or car for which the family
> longs, cannot be described as working to keep
> the wolf from the door. Yet she is working to give
> her children what she considers they need for
> their richest and happiest development.

The personal reasons women give for working
are as varied as they themselves are. Mrs. Eldridge,
for example, tells us she works to help with the mort-
gage payments. Mrs. Foster wants to be sure there'll
be enough put away for the children's college education. Mrs. Shaw's salary goes toward the support
of her parents. Mrs. Jerome thinks the children will
profit from summers at camp. And Mrs. Field knows
that the whole family benefits from the trips to
Europe her added income makes possible.

To assume that money is the only reason for
working is to oversimplify human motivation. On the

other hand, to consider monetary reasons ignoble is to ignore reality. It is hardly news that a reasonable amount of money is essential to family security and happiness, although naturally what one family feels is reasonable, another may consider inadequate.

One mother wants to buy a good painting to fill the space the living room wall seems to be crying out for. Another knows her salary will make piano lessons possible for her daughter. Still another likes to add to the family library and enlarge the record collection. Necessities or extras? The words obviously mean different things to different families. By dint of mothers' working, American families now have purchasing power which stretches to include a good deal that makes life better for them than it would otherwise have been.

But many mothers who work do so for more than their pay check, important though that is. Mrs. Eldridge takes pride in a job well done—in sharpening her actuarial skills and increasing her knowledge of the insurance field. Exchanges of views with her colleagues at the office are a source of pleasure and satisfaction to Mrs. Foster. Housekeeping is simply not a full-time job for Mrs. Shaw now that the children are in school—just as Mrs. Jerome needs a respite from endless talk of the Beatles. And Mrs. Field considers it wasteful not to use her superb education outside her home as well as in it.

The need to feel useful outside the home, to

grow and develop, to be part of a larger world, to use one's abilities—all these, plus the tangible recognition of a salary, make up the variety of motives that underlie a mother's decision to take a job. If she does *not* want a paid job, a mother's decision is just as personal in its reasons, just as valid in its conclusions, just as unassailable in its right to ignore public opinion.

# 2

## DOUBLE YOUR PLEASURE,
## DOUBLE THEIR FUN?

BEFORE deciding to work outside the home you will naturally consider the feelings and attitudes of the people who are important in your life—your husband and your children first, and then perhaps even your neighbors and close relatives, especially if their co-operation is to be a factor in your taking a job.

### DOES IT MATTER
### WHAT YOUR HUSBAND THINKS?

The double job is virtually impossible if your husband is against the idea. If he isn't all for it, forget it. Those who have studied the problem extensively

32

state flatly that a husband's cooperation is crucial to the success or failure of the employed homemaker. Without his moral support (at the very least), the emotional cost of attempting to manage a double job would be too great. Someone is bound to suffer— and chances are the someone would be you.

But for the most part today's husbands can and do accept their wives' working without feeling either resentful or threatened, and many cheer on their wives' career ambitions with pride and enthusiasm. With the old pattern of "dominant husband-subservient wife" on the wane, the new husband-wife relationship emerges more clearly as a partnership. Still and all, this does not mean that if you decide to take a job, you should transfer your domestic responsibilities to your husband. (Sensing that this might be in the cards for them may explain why some husbands are not too eager to see their wives go out to work.)

A recent survey made of men whose wives combined jobs with homemaking revealed that 80% of the husbands expressed approval of their wives' working. This favorable attitude did not hold when men with non-working wives were polled. The most encouraging conclusion to be drawn from this fact is that the husbands of wives with jobs had the first-hand experience of knowing that things could turn out satisfactorily.

"Man's best possession," wrote Euripides, "is a sympathetic wife." Sympathy works both ways. One

husband, who had encouraged his wife's career ambitions, said recently: "It sounds funny, but now
that my wife's back at a job she seems to enjoy housework. Before, she fought it all the time. But these
days I've even caught her singing as she does the
dishes."

The wife herself reported that her whole attitude
had changed since going back to her job as a hospital
technician. "I became a technician in the first place,"
she said, "because I liked the work. I didn't suddenly *stop* liking it because I had a family. My husband understands this, and it's true that I now do a
better job at home and at the lab, too."

Another wife, whose husband had suggested that
she take a part-time job, told us this story: "In my
pre-working days when my husband came home
from work, I would meet him at the door ready to
dump all responsibility into his hands. On evenings
he was late, I felt even more oppressed by my day,
crammed as usual with tedious and insignificant decisions. I wanted to unload them all because they
were getting me nowhere, merely weighing me down.

"I realize that the decisions I make at work
could be seen that way, too, if they were all I had.
But knowing that my job belongs to a larger world
outside brings me a lot of satisfaction. And it's ma-
terially rewarding, too. My job at home is equally
real and fulfilling—it has the long-range satisfactions
of watching my children grow and develop."

And her husband, who had provided the impetus for her return to work, added: "I knew she'd be happy once she got into the swing again." Asked if he didn't think the two jobs tired her out, he answered: "They haven't so far—quite the contrary; but I'd rather come home any day to a tired wife than, Heaven forbid, a tiresome one."

Parenthetically, but most importantly, fatigue is not the common complaint of employed mothers. At-home mothers, however, often list it as their chief grievance. It is seen so frequently in doctors' offices that it bears the popular label "housewife's fatigue." Many physicians, finding nothing organically wrong with these housewife-patients, conclude that the basic cause of their fatigue, as well as assorted aches and pains, is nothing more than overwhelming boredom.

Many a busy working woman insists that combining housework with an interesting outside job makes her feel fully alive. No, the children don't bore her. No, every phase of housekeeping is not uncreative drudgery. But the repetitiveness of most housework, coupled with a dearth of adult companionship often *can* be deadly. Frequently all it takes to recharge the generators is a satisfying job. When the children are well cared for, being separated from them for a part of the day only makes coming home to them that much more enjoyable. It is highly possible that the children may feel the same way too.

## HOW NOT TO SHORT-CHANGE HIM

You simply must talk things out completely with your husband before taking a job. Fran Nielsen's husband Joe was somewhat reluctant at first to have her go to work. He felt, understandably, that his comforts might be neglected if she took on a job. "It was bad enough to know that the children were claiming most of her attention," he complained, only half in jest, "when suddenly comes the suggestion that she go back to work." Later Joe was forced to admit: "I didn't think she could manage two jobs. But I was wrong—she handles both, it seems, more easily than one."

How did Fran Nielsen accomplish this without short-changing anyone—Joe, the children, or herself? Like most mothers who work and manage a home as well, she was fully aware of Joe's attitude and brought up the topic often for discussion before any decisions were made. "Look," she told Joe when the idea first took hold, "you know this job is something I'd love to get back to, but we have to face the fact that if I do take it, perhaps a few things you care about will occasionally be overlooked. We may run out of butter some morning. Or I might have to delay sewing a button back on your shirt. Think we can work this out?"

And, of course, subjects much more important than these were talked over. Basic matters were not too hard to iron out—the household help, the children's schedules, the money matters. But more subtle questions were also discussed. Joe disclosed that washing dishes would make him feel like a sissy, though he wouldn't mind vacuuming one little bit, if that would help. Although he barely tolerated food-shopping, he agreed to go along with Fran one night a week—just to make sure of the butter supply, he said. Fran rarely asked Joe to take on other domestic duties, knowing that sooner or later he would come to resent his "double burden." It is interesting to note that she did not apply the term "double burden" to her own dual role, and never really thought of it that way. Like most mothers who want to work, she accepted both jobs with relish.

Probably the best and most realistic appraisal of a successful husband-wife relationship in which both work is this one related by Mirra Komarovsky in her book *Women in the Modern World:*

My husband is proud of my career. The moment I receive some good news, a salary raise, say, I rush to the phone to tell him. But I know that part of his unalloyed joy comes from the fact that my raises do not threaten his superiority in earning capacity. My salary is a sizable addition to our income, and he feels more secure because both of us can earn. At the same time, it doesn't disturb the stereotype, which I find comfortable, of the husband being the chief provider . . . I am sure that my career hasn't undermined *his* ambition. He is naturally ambitious and quite aggressive and needs a sense of accomplishment. While I am as open about my ambitions as anyone can hope to be, now and then, reading his mind, I play down a little triumph. Occasionally he is not too unhappy about some little failure of mine, and to hear his chuckle, I even play it up. It is interesting, though, that it doesn't work the other way; that is, that he never needs to play down some business scoop and never has to back up my ego by disparaging himself . . . [My] writing assignments cannot always fit into the regular schedule. Why does he put up with it? Because he is resourceful and has many interests to occupy him of an evening if I am busy; because he respects my job and likes the prestige and the color it brings into his life; because, despite my hard work, I am not competitive or aggressive and in relations with me he feels secure; because many qualities give him compensating areas of superiority. To conclude, I think that his account of our marriage would substantially agree with mine.

## UNCOVER HIDDEN FEELINGS

When examining attitudes (your own as well as your husband's) about your going to work, you may discover that they are not always what they first appear to be. Human motivation is subtle and complex. Some men say they are against having their wives work because they consider it a personal affront and a reflection on their ability to provide. This attitude may stem from a husband's own particular feeling that he is not adequate to the demands of marriage and the responsibilities of a household. He may worry about what his friends and neighbors will think of him, especially if it is uncommon in his circle for wives to work.

A wife's working may signify a subconscious feeling that her husband cannot care for her and the children in the way other husbands do. Some working mothers use their jobs as weapons or alibis. A woman with a tendency toward martyrdom finds her responsibilities overwhelming with two jobs, even though she herself insists on working. A wife for whom sex is a problem can offer "proof" that she is too tired from her double duties to enjoy it. A woman who feels uneasy as a hostess will surely find it harder than ever to find the time to entertain once she has a job. The list of "excuses" could be extended endlessly.

A working career undertaken in the face of these attitudes (no matter what the rationalizations) is unlikely to yield any positive or long-range gains. When deep-seated resentments are present in a husband-wife relationship, they can erupt under a variety of situations, and too often the wife's job becomes the convenient scapegoat—all blame is laid to it. But it is rarely, if ever, the job alone that is the underlying cause of trouble. If seeking a job brought to the surface angry feelings already existing in a precarious

marriage, it could well be the kindest jolt the couple
ever encountered. Insights gained from mutual discussion or from therapy might uncover the reasons
for hostility and put the relationship on a firmer
basis. Both husband and wife could then be helped
to work toward the fulfillment of one another.

## WILL IT HURT THE KIDS?

No mother feels free about going to work if she is not
reasonably certain that her children are being well
taken care of during her absence. The Children's
Bureau has this to say:

> Other things being equal, we think that few
> mothers of children under six—and fewer mothers
> of children under three—are able to carry a *full-
> time* job and also fill the needs of their children
> in these crucial and vulnerable early years. But
> other things are not always equal.

The italics are ours, and they are worth thinking about. *Full-time* jobs are generally not the answer
for most mothers of young children, but *part-time*
work often is, especially if youngsters are in nursery
schools for half a day, or if there is a satisfactory substitute to take over while the mother is away from
home. ("Satisfactory substitutes" are a big order, and
we look into them in detail in Chapter III.) Part-

time work allows the mother of young children to eat her cake and have it, too. While not missing out on the endless delights of the pre-school years, the mother who takes a part-time job gains valuable and continuing work experience that is bound to make the road back to full-time employment easier later on. The double job is not easy when the children are young, but many mothers who are able to combine the two feel they are better mothers for that very reason. When a mother, no matter how loving, is kept from doing work that means a great deal to her, she may very well hold it against her children, consciously or not.

Every mother who has a job outside the house or is thinking of taking one asks herself if it will be bad for the children. So much has been said—pro and con—that it's no wonder answers seem doubtful and confusing. And of course, there is no one answer. You are not a carbon copy of your neighbor, and your family's needs and problems are uniquely your own. For years, nearly all professionals in the fields of child psychology and family relations were as vigorously opposed to mothers working as were many uninformed laymen who had nothing but their own prejudices to go on. Since the opinions of these experts were not arrived at lightly, they merited the widespread attention they received. So vociferously were their views first propounded (and subsequently quoted and re-quoted in the popular press) that echoes of them reverberate to this day whenever the topic comes up.

But when we re-examine the data upon which these experts originally built their anti-working case, we realize how inapplicable they are, today. The strong professional disapproval stemmed originally from studies of families who were disorganized and unstable even before the mothers went to work. In other words, the personality disturbances in children which the experts noted and worried about did not arise from the simple fact alone that mothers were employed. Much more important was the disrupted and unhappy family situation from which the children came and the inadequate substitute care they received. Thus working mothers acquired the dubious reputation which lingers on, despite new evidence and changed circumstances.

Now that so many mothers of stable families have worked and have brought up happy and healthy children, we are in a position to re-evaluate the earlier findings. We know that the element of maternal employment, considered by itself alone, does not determine whether a child will be disturbed. According to Dr. Eleanor E. Maccoby, there are other factors—his intellectual and physical capacity, the kind of community he's raised in, the emotional stability of his parents—which weigh heavily in his development. Whether or not his mother works is only a single—and sometimes awfully small—factor.

New studies go on all the time. In an excellent textbook, *The Employed Mother in America,* F. Ivan Nye and Lois Wladis Hoffman have brought together research findings of sociologists, psychologists, economists, and others from 1957 to early 1962. These experts are more cautious, perhaps more sophisticated than were those of an earlier day. Practically no one reports that working *per se* is bad for children, nor yet that it has no effect at all.

In analyzing other major research on the subject, Stanford University's Dr. Lois Meek Stolz has this to say:

> When one concludes a study of this kind, one is impressed with the number of different and opposing findings which research concerning the effect of maternal employment on children has produced. One can say almost anything one desires about the children of employed mothers and support the statement by some research study.

### TUNING IN TO THEM

Obviously it is impossible to generalize about children's attitudes toward their mother's working. Many factors are involved—the age of the child, his temperament, his special needs. But one thing is certain: no child is going to be happy if he feels his mother is more interested in her *job* than in *him*. A mother knows full well that this is not the case, but unless she is on guard against such an implication, it might be easy for the child to imagine it to be true.

One mother, engrossed in a research job for an advertising agency, suddenly realized that she had devoted most of her spare thought for the past week to the assignment. Some of the time she wasn't even "hearing" Eddie, her five-year-old.

"It worked fine on one level," she said, "because I could shut out the yells and normal squabbles of Eddie and his pals playing outside in the back yard. The real secret, though, is to know when to come up for communication.

"You might say that I was a little like my friend who had a serious hearing handicap for several years before consenting to wear a hearing aid. Her children were the ones most pleased by her new responsiveness. They would come up to her and say, 'Mom, are you tuned in? I want to ask you something.' As for me, I was positive I was always tuned in to Eddie, but on a Sunday afternoon, when he said in an exasperated tone, 'Mom, when I speak to you, you are supposed to talk back to me,' I was brought up short. Here I was—letting the assignment take over at home too, and I'd been the one who had assured my husband I could juggle both home and job without another thought. I guess what I'm saying is that thought calls for many different wave lengths."

## SEEING IS BELIEVING

Knowing what you do at work, why it is important to you, and visiting your office—all influence the attitudes your children are likely to adopt toward your working. After Shirley Collins had been back at work in a brokerage office for a month, she decided that *talking* about her job to her three children hadn't been enough. The next step was for them to see for themselves. She made arrangements for her children (one at a time) to visit the office, meet her co-workers, and learn more about where and how she worked. Right away, her job became more real to them. On the days she worked, they knew she was not taking off for a vast Nowhere but going to a definite Office, full of friendly people and interesting equipment.

"Taking them with me in a group wouldn't have worked so well," Mrs. Collins told us. "It would have been just another outing, like a trip to the museum. On an individual basis I let each child drift toward the aspect of my job that interested him. He could then feel more directly connected with it. Each went home and described his own reaction to the other two. My youngest, the third-grader, could hardly wait to tell his class about it the next day. They're all as proud of me—each in his own way—as I am of them. I couldn't get as much satisfaction as I do out of this job if I weren't certain that Hank and the kids were for it."

"When I first started back to work, Anne, my nine-year-old, acted strangely," another mother told us. "Even though she loved our housekeeper, on days that I was not home by 3:30 when the bus deposited her, she would stamp her feet and refuse to change into her play clothes. I almost gave up my job, but I thought it would be better for us both in the long run to try to work it out. Anne's father thought so, too. I think Anne's behavior was caused partly because she has always hated any change in routine and partly because I hadn't talked things out with her well enough in advance. She never really felt involved in what I was doing. I began bringing home interesting layouts I was working on at the office, and I explained something about them to Anne. This led to our discussing many things, but the most important thing we ever talked about was how Anne felt. I encouraged her to bring all her feelings—good and bad—out into the open. Anne is basically a happy child, with many friends and interests of her own, but she did need frequent reassurance at the beginning that I didn't prefer the office to her. Several weeks after our first talk, Anne's teacher assigned her a rather complicated project about Latin America, and I helped Anne organize it. I was also able to track down some visual map devices at the office which I brought home to her. Imagine how delighted I felt when Anne pointed out to me the similarity of her project to some of my own work. From then on, she was really sold on my career!"

By and large, children whose own activities are taken seriously respond with the same seriousness to their parents' work. When they themselves are respected, they can respect the fact that Mother has a right to interests of her own. Given their rightful share of attention, they can share in their mother's job and be proud of it. After all, children do want their parents to keep up with their world's changes, to know the score. The daughter of a small-town hospital technician found a real purpose in taking chemistry. English was more than just a required subject for the junior high school son of a free-lance writer. Math became more meaningful when Jane's mother took her to visit the office where she worked two days a week as a securities analyst.

### BRIEF ENCOUNTERS

If a mother could be in two places at once (and every mother wishes that many times in her life), she would be at home for that one important moment when the children come in from school.

Usually the pattern is sweet and snappy: "Hi, mom, I'm taking off! Betsy's waiting for me—okay?

See you later." The time for communication may be only an instant, but every child likes his mother to be waiting for him, doing nothing more than just being there. Giving up this extremely short moment of company, however, need not be earth-shattering if there is a warm, friendly substitute to take over. Susan's can't-wait confidences usually *do* wait until dinner time because Susan has a date with Betsy that can't wait, either.

In terms of actual conversation time, mother and child often talk more when she times her afternoon coffee break to coincide with the child's return home and calls him on the phone. Today's children have one finger on a telephone dial practically from birth —they realize you are within immediate reach if they need to talk to you.

Remember, too, that mothers who stay home all the time don't commune with their children constantly. The times of meaningful exchange are few and all the more precious because of that. The difference is that mothers who go to work cannot always wait for those moments to happen so they try to create an encouraging climate for them at all times.

### FAVORS FOR ALL

When a mother returns to a job after having been home for a while, many older children, too, resent this changed state of affairs at first. A youngster may express his initial displeasure in any number of ways, depending on his age and personality. The twelve-year-old daughter of a returning secretary-mother sulked most evenings on the days her mother worked. Reassured by the family's physician that her daughter's reaction was not serious and could not possibly last very long, the mother decided that the time for self-recrimination had passed. Instead of continuing to blame herself, she instituted a simple form of treatment: bribery. "Half the money I get from my next paycheck I'll put in your bank account," she told her daughter. "Then when you decide what kind of puppy you want, we'll go out and get him."

No miracle drug ever worked faster or better. "I know some parents would be against the idea," the mother said, "but in our case it worked wonders. Karen immediately saw a purpose in my going to work—obviously her purpose wasn't the same as mine —but from then on her acceptance of my job was complete. She could see the tangible results, and that's important."

Karen's mother also decided not to slight the small favors which meant much to both Karen and to her father. She always made a special effort to work them into her busy day, even at the expense of other matters which *she* considered more worthwhile. For instance, if she had to make a choice, she baked Karen's special chocolate cake instead of polishing the silver. Or, having time for only one errand, she picked up hair tonic for her husband rather than flowers for the living room.

It is not always easy for mothers to interpret the various expressions of disapproval children exhibit. Is the misbehavior temporary? Is it serious? Should I ignore it? Questions like these go through the mind of every mother whose child acts up in one way or another on her return to work. It is a good plan to discuss any unfavorable reactions your child may have with your pediatrician or with some other professional person who knows your youngster well. Your own emotional involvement makes it difficult for you to make an objective appraisal. Normal children from stable households generally adapt very well; their upsets, like Karen's, are short-term and easily taken care of. Others reactions may have deeper significance. In any event, you will want to know as much as you can for certain, so that you can handle the situation wisely.

### WHAT WILL THE NEIGHBORS SAY?

Is it possible that the idea of your holding a job with the blessings of your husband and children could be gradually undermined by the attitude of a neighbor or a relative? Probably not. You would not be likely to reverse a healthy decision that has been carefully arrived at and that works well for you and your family. Of course, if you are a mother whose guilt at leaving her children is overwhelming, you'll be certain to go into a tailspin if your sister-in-law makes a disparaging remark about "mothers who ought to be at home looking after their children." If your decision to work is clouded by anxiety, words of disapproval from another mother at a PTA meeting can upset your equilibrium more than momentarily. But if you know that your job is right for you and your family, the words will slide off your back unnoticed. You may even see through their surface meaning into . . . could it be envy?

If you value your neighbors' opinions a great deal, you might want to bring up the subject of working mothers at the next *kaffee klatsch* and state your point of view. (If you are already working, you probably won't have time for the neighborly visits, and in truth avoiding them might be one big reason you decided to go back to work in the first place.) The pressures to conform are intense these days, and if you live in a tightly-knit community whose values are different from yours, you have a built-in opportunity to demonstrate to your children that you and your husband are not afraid to be yourselves, to have your own standards and to stick by them. With good feeling and with respect for the opinions of others, you still have the responsibility to let your youngsters know where you stand. "This is how *we* do it. This is what *we* believe. We don't necessarily have to be like the Jacksons next door or the Bromleys up the street."

To sum up, most studies made about children's attitudes toward their mothers as workers reveal clearly that if the parents' attitudes are in favor, so, too, are the youngsters'. Knowing that thousands and thousands of mothers are handling their jobs capably will help you to assess the attitudes of those who are important in your life. Some of the negative comments you may encounter from friends or neighbors may be based on nothing more solid than ignorance. Or prejudice. Or, as we suggested, envy.

Like most mothers everywhere, working mothers love their children and want to do their best for them. And with careful planning and judicious juggling, they are managing successfully. It is unfortunate that the whole question often turns into a tug-of-war with mother in the middle. One side shouts "Go home!" while the other side yells "Get out!" No matter what a mother does, there's bound to be a sniper on the sidelines. But this is no time to be frightened and run for cover. If the pattern of living that suits you and your family best includes a job for you, chances are good that you can manage your dual role very well. No one in his right mind would claim that it is a breeze, but millions have proved that it can be done. There are lessons to be learned from the experiences of the many normal mothers of healthy families who have worked and who have reared wholesome chil-

dren, too. And the most important lesson has to do
with the substitute who will stand in for you when
you are at work. What should you look for? What
qualities ought she to have? What kind of arrangements are likely to work out best?

# 3

## NOT A "MOTHER-SUBSTITUTE," BUT A MOTHER-HELPER

WHETHER you're planning to take a part-time job because your youngster is only three or four, or concidering something full-time because your children are older, the question of who pinch hits while you're gone still remains paramount. It would be tempting to profile the ideal mother-substitute, but wouldn't it also be a little absurd? You know—perhaps to your own dismay—that no perfect parent exists. It's hardly news that no perfect substitute exists either. A lengthy check-list of qualifications will not help you to uncover some improbable paragon. However, conscientious mothers do try to choose people to take over

54

for them whose views and methods are not unlike their own. (A study of the arrangements made by working mothers in Spokane, Washington, in the spring of 1958 revealed what had generally been assumed: that the substitutes' treatment of the children was not radically different from what the youngsters would have received from their mothers, had they not been working. A conscientious mother, in other words, is likely to get a conscientious substitute.)

### BE FIRM FROM THE BEGINNING

Naturally, you want your helper to be a warm, friendly person who can be flexible, understanding, and responsive to a child's genuine needs. Just as your employer sets the policies of his business, it's up to you to instruct your stand-in in your own policies of child rearing. It is much better to do this at the outset in a firm and friendly manner than to feel intimidated and perhaps reluctant to make your position clear later on. It should be understood that when questions come up which your helper does not know how to handle, she should defer giving the children an answer until she can consult with you. But on ordinary day-to-day decisions (how much TV, for example) which you both have discussed and agreed on, you will want to back her up so as to give her confidence and, equally important, not upset the children. Youngsters are adaptable—it doesn't hurt them to have to be a little tidier or a bit more helpful— so even if your substitute does not do things exactly as you do, no harm is likely to result unless, of course, she is an "over"-overseer—overstrict or overpermissive. But then if she were too inflexible to adapt to your child-rearing pattern, you wouldn't want her to care for your youngster anyway.

No one can be expected to fill your shoes completely. But being separated from your children for a number of hours each week does not mean that you have abdicated your parental role. You are still the one most concerned with, most interested in, most necessary to your youngsters. It is possible, however, to find a substitute who is good with children in general and who takes a genuine interest in your youngsters in particular. For some, that substitute will be a housekeeper. Others may have a mother or mother-in-law who can take over, or a friend or neighbor.

### IF YOURS IS A PRE-SCHOOL CHILD

As yet neither the quality nor the quantity of nursery education in this country begin to meet the need for it. (In the chapter that follows we discuss nursery schools, day-care centers, and after-school programs.) But even if there is a good nursery school in your neighborhood and your child seems ready for it, you cannot just send him off happily and then relax in a part-time job, secure in the knowledge that this one particular problem has been dealt with. You will still need someone to take over for you when you are not available or when your child catches those inevitable sniffles and must stay home. If your stand-in is a grandmother or a neighbor or someone else whom your child knows and trusts, you are in luck. But if you are taking your first post-motherhood job, you may not have had any long-term experience with a permanent substitute. It is tremendously important for a younger child, especially, to become friendly with and rely on the person who will be in charge when you are away. Therefore do not consider it an extravagance (it is more than worth it for your peace of mind) to hire someone who will report for work at least a half a dozen times while you are still at home. Giving your child a chance to get used to someone new and observing how they get on together will help to relieve any home-directed anxieties that may pop up once you are at work. Knowing that the arrangement is working out will make your double job easier on everyone. And, of course, if it is not to be, you will be able to tell that in advance, too. You may need to look for someone else, or you may decide that your child is not yet ready to be left with *any* substitute.

No evidence exists to prove that pre-school children from healthy families are emotionally damaged when their mothers go to work if good helpers take over their care. This does not mean that a young child does not require a good deal of "mothering," but it need not come from his mother alone. In analyzing current attitudes on the subject, Elizabeth Herzog of the Children's Bureau says:

> There is among many who work with children a strong conviction that it is damaging to an infant or a very young child to have more than one "mother figure" at a time, or in a sequence. This principle has been challenged by some anthropologists who point to the frequency of "assistant mothers" in primitive societies and the absence of evidence that children, or the adults they become, are harmed by it. Mothers often leave children to be cared for by other adults or older children while they work in the fields. Since the custom is universal in the groups that practice it, say the anthropologists, one would have to conclude either that the society itself is "sick" or that the children survive the mother's daily absence without perceptible damage.

Mrs. Derby went back to her field when her child was a little over three. Before her marriage she had been a successful decorator and when she had an opportunity to rejoin her old firm on a part-time basis, she weighed the pros and cons with her husband and chose to return. Instead of sending Janie, who was rather a shy child, to nursery school, Mrs. Derby decided to let her stay home. She felt comfortable about doing so because she had a reliable maid who had been with the family for some time. This arrangement worked out well, and the following year when Janie joined the nursery group, she thoroughly enjoyed her school experience. And Mrs. Derby thoroughly enjoyed her part-time job—an enjoyment which communicated itself to Janie. There were never any anxious good-byes and no appeasing maneuvers that might well have upset Janie.

On the other hand, when Mrs. Crane thought she wanted to go back to work, she had no hesitancy about enrolling four-year-old Mark in nursery school. He hit it off beautifully the very first day, and if anything, liked school even better as time went on. He also liked his sitter. Everything would probably have worked out well had Mrs. Crane taken the time to question herself before she took a job, and be confident that working was right for her. She had simply had a vague feeling that it would be nice, but she was not quite sure. And Mark, like all children, reacted to his mother's uncertainties. Sensing her doubts, he exploited them by demanding a present every day. He balked at going to bed at his usual time and began to raise objections to nearly everything. Afraid that she was jeopardizing Mark's security, Mrs. Crane quit her job after the second month.

These two cases are cited simply to point out that there is no rule of thumb by which you can determine what is right for your family. You and your husband know each other and your children better than anyone else does. You know what resources your community offers. You know what your neighbors are like and what cooperation they are likely to offer. You know your own situation, your own needs, your own wishes. Once you have determined that working is the best course for you, your feeling right about it is basic. If you do not, your own guilt or uneasiness, besides making you miserable, will be reflected in the behavior of your children and the reaction and attitude of your husband. When you choose to work, you must be able to do so happily and with conviction.

For a time, when you first start to work, you may find that your children are especially demanding, clinging or unruly when you come home. Even though they get on well in nursery school and are happy with their sitter, sometimes at the sight of you they relax the emotional self-controls they have managed during the day. This is almost always temporary; but at the beginning, you and your husband may need to be more flexible in the standards you set as well as more tolerant of the children's inordinate demands on your time. This phase, if it does occur, disappears quickly as children adjust to change. Obviously, they won't adjust if they feel neglected—whether you go out to work or to play golf.


## IF HE'S IN SCHOOL ALREADY

Just because your child is in school and often acts so self-contained and independent, you are not fooled—you know full well he is not nearly ready to be on his own. Even though he's accounted for from around 8:30 A.M. to 3 P.M., you still have to plan for those after-school hours if your working day extends beyond that time.

Mrs. Allen, for example, has her two boys—aged seven and nine—go to her next door neighbor's house after school. The boys consider it their headquarters for the hour before their mother gets home. In exchange, Mrs. Allen pays the neighbor a modest weekly sum—and baby-sits for her one evening a week.

Mrs. Baer, on the other hand, entrusts her eight-year-old daughter, Sue, to a reliable, mature college student, who welcomes her home from school and supervises her homework. Sue knows it is all right to have schoolmates in or to visit a friend occasionally, if her sitters knows her whereabouts and if an adult is at the friend's house to look after the children.

Mrs. Kersten is lucky because her mother-in-law, still young and vigorous, has taken a small apartment nearby. The children vary their after-school routine. On Mondays and Thursdays they go to their grandmother's house. On the other days Grandma is waiting at their own house for them.

Some women, like Mrs. Duncan, are able to employ a housekeeper who also doubles as a mother-helper. Mrs. Duncan's helper comes at noon, five days a week. She cleans house, sends the laundry out, does the marketing, and looks after the youngsters when they come home from school. She also starts the evening meal so that after Mrs. Duncan adds the finishing touches, there is always time for pre-dinner fun and confidences . . . and even some of the inevitable arguing that makes real families different from and more interesting than the idealized images of them in TV commercials.

Even when a child's after-school hours are adequately taken care of, there are crises that crop up in every family. Johnny's throat is sore, and he has to stay home. The school nurse telephones to report that Josephine has an earache. Suzanne comes down with the mumps. When it's nothing serious, most women depend on their housekeeper or relative or friend to carry on as usual. Nevertheless, all working mothers have to think ahead and plan ahead to make certain there is someone capable of "covering" on short notice, when necessary. In many households, the older children (provided *they're* not the ones with the earaches) can pitch in after school and help out considerably.

## HOW YOUR TEEN-AGERS CAN HELP

Why not rely on them to supervise the younger ones now and then? There is certainly nothing wrong in encouraging the older ones to assume more responsibility. (Maybe it will even help to end the epidemic of books and articles on the irresponsibility of today's youth.) Even if you were not working, it would not be good for your adolescent children to have you on tap for them 100% of the time, available always to run their errands and pick up after them. But, of course, you do not want to go to the opposite extreme and expect too much. Teen-agers have their own work and interests and cannot be expected to take over completely. They can relieve your paid helper occasionally and they can and should be required to take on some specific chores. (Even the younger ones can be given appropriate work to do, as we discuss in Chapter VII.) A reasonable and flexible assignment of tasks is perfectly well in order. It might serve to offset the very real disadvantages for youngsters from no longer having the clear-cut family functions expected of them in the past. While not imposing on your teenager, you will still be asking enough of him to engender a feeling of pride in his contributions to

**64**

the welfare of the family . . . and perhaps to his own
financial status as well. (A few extra shekels now
and then as a token of appreciation for *extra* chores
stand very little chance of being refused.)


## GUILTY, OR NOT?

Even if a mother feels right about working, she may
have a twinge of guilt about it now and then.
(Thought-provoker: there seem to be no reports of
guilt feelings in non-working mothers who are occu-
pied with community affairs much of the day and
often spend no more time with their children than
do business or professional mothers.)

You would not be human if you did not have
at least an occasional worry about whether your
stand-in is really as good as she should be. But that
does not mean that every time a problem arises you
must automatically leap to the conclusion that your
job is the reason for it. Non-working mothers are
far from problemless. In fact, they have been rather
articulate lately about their own stay-at-home pressures and frustrations, as well as their difficulties with
their young.

The main thing to guard against is trying to com-
pensate for your absence by overindulging your
youngsters or fearing to take a firm stand with them
when it is needed. Even though you want the hours
spent with your children to be as happy and pleasant

as possible, you cannot close your eyes to misbehavior: you have to set limits and establish rules which your children can accept and follow. Otherwise, you risk confusing them, as well as your stand-in. In the long run, your youngsters will feel more secure, and more certain of your love and interest in them, because they know you care enough to set reasonable limits. And they need very much to feel that you care deeply about them and their concerns—their friends, their hobbies, their life at school.

You may not have time to be as active in school affairs or parent-teacher groups as some other parents. But for certain school events even the most loving substitute will not do. You yourself will simply have to take time from work, if necessary, to visit the school on special days—not that you won't want to, anyway. You can also attend evening meetings so that your youngster knows how much you care about his activities and his accomplishments in school. When you are able to supply cookies for a parents' meeting or a grade party or assist with some school program, you get to know the school staff your child comes in contact with, his classmates and their parents, and feel more in touch with the situation generally. This gives you an additional bond with your child, one of activity as well as your natural interest . . . keeps you and your child comfortably tuned in to one another.

It is a truism that the *quality* of the relationship between a mother and child is what counts, not the *quantity* of time spent together. Your relationship with your children obviously does not depend solely upon the number of hours you spend together. Time together *is* important—but your influence stretches beyond this. The feeling of being together can prevail even during the hours of separation. Your children know you will be home at a certain time, and that they can always turn to you when life seems tough or complex or marvelously exciting. Coming home to an empty house, where there is no one to take an interest in him, is not good for any child. But so long as someone is there who truly cares about him —your paid stand-in, a family volunteer, a neighbor— he can learn to postpone the pleasure of seeing and being with you. He looks forward to your companionship and the evening family get-togethers just as all youngsters do, perhaps more so than many who think of Mom mainly as an ever-present fixture, not unlike the kitchen stove.

## TOO MUCH TOGETHERNESS

Even with a reliable helper and plenty of evidence that the children are doing well, working mothers sometimes wonder if there is enough *family* togetherness. Perhaps we have all been drugged by this togetherness happy-pill and have lost track of the important fact that each human being inhabits a separate world of his own—and that if he is to inhabit that world successfully, there are many things he must do alone and on his own. A child needs to sit back from his family now and then and let his experiences soak in, to judge their value and his reactions to them.

The fact is, children need to be alone occasionally —"let alone," that is, not "left alone," in order to discover and search themselves for impulse, inclination, ambition, and opinion, however tenuous these abstract qualities may be in the beginning. They need to assess and enjoy achievement, to face and appraise failure. They need to develop that genuine individuality and self-acceptance which alone protect one from the twin dangers of meaningless rebellion and cowed conformity. Although it is vital for families to be together and for children to be with their parents, each hour of separation need not be considered a loss. Apartness is often a necessary ingredient for growth. For some, it is even a luxury that is not easily come by.

Togetherness need not be interpreted so literally, after all. If you work where you can lift the phone and call home occasionally, you can be comfortably in touch with your children. A regular telephone call when the children come home from school helps them know that you are thinking about them even while you are at work. And, of course, your substitute must know that she can get in touch with you whenever it is necessary.

If you can, you will want to arrange to have your child phone you when he needs to. Perhaps he simply cannot wait to tell you that he made the team or got an A in English, or perhaps he just needs to unload a gripe or two. And don't worry—if he is busy and active and happy, he is unlikely to develop an acute case of telephonitis.

Try, as we suggested earlier, to arrange for your youngster to pay a brief visit to your place of work. It will help him to visualize what goes on when you are away from him. He might even be able to bring to school something tangible connected with what you do—a sketch, a report, a small office instrument—and become the star of Show and Tell.

### BITING THE HAND THAT FEEDS YOUR CHILDREN

One of the hardest things for a working mother to take is the jealousy that she is bound to feel if her child becomes increasingly attached to the substitute who cares for him. It is only natural for a mother to feel rivalrous if she hears her child say, "No, I'd rather have Mary help me than you." It is not a very comfortable predicament. Mother is caught in the middle. On the one hand, she is pleased that her stand-in is working out satisfactorily. On the other, she is certain to be somewhat resentful. How can this dilemma be faced? A good beginning is to realize that the reaction is perfectly natural and nothing to be ashamed of. When you keep in mind the possibility of its happening and are able to recognize it for what it is, your jealousy may not disappear but you will be able to handle it better.

Some mothers, unable or unwilling to acknowledge their own jealousy, instead take to criticizing their stand-in, picking on some minor failing and enlarging on it. (This is known as biting the hand that feeds your children.) Others rationalize by insisting that their child is becoming too close to the substitute. They then come to a decision that the relationship is unhealthy and must stop for the good of the child. Neither of these reactions, though understandable, is helpful to you, your child, or your stand-in.

It may cheer you to reflect that as a youngster gets older, he often needs an adult friend with whom he can talk freely. In earlier days when large families with many children and many adults lived under the same wide roof, responsibility for child-rearing was spread thin among the adults. Then every child had an adult ally, other than his parents, to whom he could turn whenever he felt he needed to. Your substitute can fill that important role today. Through your understanding, you can make it possible for your youngster to confide in another grownup when he needs to without any sense of disloyalty to you.

Once you have found a good substitute, you will certainly want to make her working conditions so pleasant that you stand a good chance of keeping her. Don't fret if her grammar isn't perfect, or her accent is odd—the kids will eventually copy you. What is vital in a mother-helper is a warm feeling for children and some reasonable assurance that she is going to stay with you for a while. Too frequent turnovers deprive a child of a sustained relationship and make for uncomfortable periods of adjustment. But a continuing, friendly relationship with a satisfactory substitute can enrich a youngster's life.

### P.S. TO A PROBLEM

Now that there are so many vigorous older women in our population who want their outside job to be caring for children, chances of your finding someone right for you appear to be better than they were just a few years ago. But we have obviously not yet come close to facing, let alone solving, an increasingly important problem.

There is a large untapped source of potential first-rate mother stand-ins. Many older women, accustomed all their lives to the hustle and bustle of raising a family, find themselves at loose ends when their children marry and move away. Occasional visits with their grandchildren are not enough to fill the void. Some seek work in industry or in neighborhood stores, but this type of employment, not easily available anyway, is a poor substitute for the kind of life these women have enjoyed within the family. Their interests have always been deeply rooted within the framework of their homes and children.

If local communities were to initiate refresher courses in child development, children's literature, and crafts adapted to specific age groups, they would find many eager recruits. The basic skills are there, plus a wealth of valuable experience and pleasure in caring for children. An acknowledgement of some kind, upon satisfactory completion of the course, would give a sense of status to the mother-substitute role and would command higher pay. These courses could be integrated with adult education extension programs or might be conducted by local nursing groups or organized through parents' associations.

# 4

## AT HOME AWAY FROM HOME

IF YOU ASK ten mothers with jobs what they most want to do with the money they earn, five will tell you they plan to use it to finance better education for their children. A recent study revealed that in addition to the personal satisfaction their jobs gave them, more than half the employed mothers with school-age children worked to "achieve cultural, educational, and health goals for the family and the children."

Parents buying new homes often will look only at houses in districts where the public school system is known to be good. Homes listed for sale command higher prices if they are located in a "good" school district. In one Connecticut town a broker showing

houses to prospective buyers commented that he knew
of one just right for them—but they wouldn't like the
school! Had it been located only 1,000 feet over the
line, it would have been perfect. As consolation he
added that the price would have been $5,000 higher if
it had stood the thousand feet away.

More and more prospective home buyers are adding another qualification to their list of New Home
Musts: a location convenient to the mother's job.

### HOW TO TELL THE RIGHT TIME

Many mothers want to return to work when their children are in school, but the precise timing varies with
each mother and child. Some women say, "As soon as
my children are in college, I'm going back!" Some use
the grade school age as a criterion of the best time
for them to return to work. Others declare they'll go
when their youngsters are old enough to enter nursery
school. More and more women intend to keep their
hand in right through pregnancy and after birth. "I
didn't want to lose contact with the people in publish-
ing," said a free-lance manuscript editor, "so after each
of my children was born I'd telephone the office on the
way home from my six-weeks' check-up. 'I'm back in
business, please keep me in mind,' I'd say. Meeting
deadlines wasn't always a snap, but then nothing that
earns me such long-range satisfactions ever is."

"This wouldn't work for some mothers, but I find it easier to leave the children to my competent nurse when they are infants rather than later," said a librarian in Chicago. She had just returned from a two-months' maternity leave after the birth of her third child. "Babies' days consist of sleeping and eating and a little bathing, and I tend to lots of that before I go to work in the morning. We all get up fairly early and have a couple of hours of togetherness—if you'll pardon the expression—before the older children take off for school and Dick and I leave for work."

There is, however, one period in a baby's life when leaving him should be handled rather carefully. This is somewhere in the second half of the first year —the "fear of strangers" period. Babies of this age often cry and pull away when they see a new face— or even an old one they haven't seen recently. This new behavior probably indicates that the baby is better able to tell the difference between his mother and everyone else. Obviously, this would not be the time suddenly to decide to go to work unless there is no choice. If it becomes necessary to go at this time, plan to bring another "mother person" into the child's life earlier so that he may get used to her before it's time for you to start the job.

The same holds true when the mother of a one and a half to two-year-old decides to return to work. One of the reasons most nursery schools do not accept children under three is that the separation from mother is often too difficult for a young child. He, too, needs to have had some previous experience with a good "mother substitute" to smooth the way.

In general, until children are ready for school, most mothers arrange for them to be cared for at home. Sometimes two or three mothers share the responsibility. In a Boston suburb two neighbors worked out a cooperative schedule to enable both to work one day a week. The first, an expert lighting consultant, used her day to go to town to deliver her work to the architect she helped and to pick up other assignments. Her two children spent that day with her neighbor. The situation was reversed on the day *her* neighbor went to her one-day-a-week job as test administrator for a child-guidance center.

## HOMEMADE PLAY SCHOOLS

In some communities mothers have organized home-play sessions for their children with happy results for all participants. A maximum of five or six children form the unit and the mothers rotate responsibility. A typical group of five might set up the following regulations:

a) the group to meet daily from 9 to 12

b) each mother to care for her child and the four others one day per week

c) the mother-in-charge for the day to pick up the children and take them home

d) the mother-of-the-day to provide juice and crackers.

Great success has been reported with such programs. If a part-time job is available nearby, a mother might work two, three, or four mornings a week. Or she will have four mornings free for work that can be done at home. One great advantage of the program lies in preparing the children for school situations by introducing them to a small group of their own age in a home situation.

### WHAT GOES ON IN A GOOD NURSERY SCHOOL?

By the age of three or four, most children need to branch out a bit more from home, whether mother works or not. "Branching out" may simply mean spending more time in play *with* (not merely beside) other children. For more and more youngsters, however, it has come to include attending a nursery school.

In the United States, nursery schools have had a relatively short history—less than 50 years. Originally they were established by women's colleges and universities to facilitate child study and teacher education.

Two recent factors have stimulated the growth of nursery education: first, the increasing knowledge of the developmental needs of young children, and second, this burgeoning need of working mothers for daytime child care. Unfortunately, however, nursery schools (as well as day-care and after-school facilities) are still incredibly inadequate.

Before considering how to provide more and better programs, let us survey the benefits of such youngster-care. What do children get out of nursery schools? Between three and five, they need most of all to learn to get along with children of their own age. They also need to extend their knowledge about the world outside of home, to express themselves spontaneously, to feel at ease with and take direction from adults other than those in their own family. These are only a few of the benefits good nursery education can provide.

Said one father to another at a nursery school Parents' Night meeting: "Four hundred and fifty a year so that Joey can paint himself like a Red Indian and then march around beating a bongo drum. But I must admit," he concluded wryly, "the boy does have a great rhythmic sense."

To its detractors, nursery school routine sometimes seems too aimless to deserve the name of education. Appearances to the contrary, good nursery school programs are planned, though flexible. If the children appear absorbed, enthusiastic, and active, they are learning. Observing a good nursery school program can be an educational experience for parents. By noting how their youngsters and others behave in groups, by discussing what they see with other parents and with the school's teachers and director, they come to learn principles of child guidance that may usefully be carried over into their own practice at home.

At nursery school, each child is free to choose his own activities: building with blocks, experimenting with simple musical instruments, "playing house," "going shopping," observing and playing with live pets, tending plants, painting, drawing, looking at picture books, and poring over puzzles. In short, he has a chance to make full use of all the facilities available at the school, both indoors and (weather permitting) outdoors, in a group or alone. In all these activities he is constantly under the watchful eye of trained teachers and assistants, who will come to his aid if he needs them. He may spend as much or as little time at one activity as he likes, and then turn wherever his boundless curiosity and interests lead him.

A nursery school child is not left to set his own schedules entirely. There are regular times for group musical and rhythmic activities, for stories, for cleaning up, toileting, resting, snacks. His nursery school day is "framed" by the set times of arrival and departure and the routines connected with these. Arrival time includes a warm welcome by one of the teachers, help with removal of outdoor clothing, and an alert "once-over" by the teacher or a nurse to be sure he does not display any signs of illness. Departure includes a friendly farewell from the teacher, who often has a word of praise or a brief comment to make about the youngster's progress to the adult who has come to call for him.

Most nursery school programs last three hours, morning or afternoon. A few—especially those designed to accommodate the needs of mothers with full-time jobs—are all-day programs. They include a nourishing lunch and a rest or nap period in a darkened room.

### HOW TO CHOOSE THE RIGHT ONE

It helps to know the types of agencies that sponsor nursery school and other day-care programs when trying to find one for your youngster. Many are operated by private individuals and organizations; some by groups of parents on a cooperative basis.

Church groups, community centers and other voluntary social agencies, local governmental agencies and public schools, as well as colleges and universities may also be operating nursery schools in your community. Any of these institutions would be an appropriate place to begin your inquiries. A family social service agency is another excellent source of information.

Visiting and comparing nursery schools is an essential preliminary to selecting the right one. In

addition to the actual program, you will want to
know about the staff, the facilities, the health and
safety arrangements. A good nursery school has areas
for both indoor and outdoor play and provides enough
space for the children to play freely. Its equipment is
varied, safe, and sturdy. It is housed in a structure
that complies with local fire, safety, and health regulations. Furnishings, including sanitary facilities, are
scaled to small children, and there are enough for
use by all.

The staff should be headed by a director and
qualified teachers professionally trained in early childhood education. Experts say there should be two
teachers (or one teacher and one assistant) for no
more than 18 children. Good nursery schools have a
nurse on staff and a doctor on call. Teachers are warm,
enthusiastic, and patient with children; they under-
stand their young charges, and respect them.

### WHAT WILL IT COST?

The answer frequently depends on the type of organization that runs the school. If it is privately operated,
rates may run between $250-800 a year for a three-
hour session. There may be additional fees if transportation is necessary. The expenses of running a good
nursery school—structure, staff, supplies—are high.
Programs operated by churches, community centers,
public agencies, or cooperatives may be able to charge

lower fees. Scholarships or sliding fees based upon ability to pay may be offered by some.

Whatever the costs, the demand for good nursery schools in most communities far exceeds the supply. The usual practice is to interview both the mother and the child before deciding whether he is ready for nursery school, whether he would be an asset to the group—and whether there is room for him. In some areas of the country well-run nursery schools are deluged with applications far beyond their capacity. Usually the reasons for this popularity are clear and valid. The school will have an excellent staff, the fees will not be prohibitive, and there might be some sort of transportation provided, although usually at additional cost. The mother who works welcomes the latter provision and should use it as one guide to choosing the proper school. Otherwise, getting a child to school on time can mean elaborate juggling of schedules, and the aim is to reduce mechanical problems to a minimum.

## HELPING YOUR CHILD ADJUST

"I thought Margaret would be shy at nursery school," confided her mother. "She's an only child and there are no other youngsters her age in our immediate neighborhood. She's always preferred to stay close to me. That's one reason I felt nursery school would be good for her. Well, the day we went to see the school and be interviewed, I was a little apprehensive. But she took one long look around at the other kids and the toys and equipment, and her face lit up like Christmas morning. Now, when she has a cold and has to miss a day or two of school, she considers it a great deprivation."

Most children take to nursery school as Margaret did. But some need a little more time than others to get used to it. Mothers frequently stay at the school during all or part of the first day, just to reassure the child that he is not being deserted. It is important to keep in the background, however, and let him become involved in the activities. Even mothers of supposedly timid, clinging children are usually surprised and delighted at the swiftness with which their youngsters become absorbed in this new world, even to the extent of forgetting mother's presence or absence.

For the child who needs a more gradual introduction, it is important that his mother remain at the school as long as he wishes her to. She can also help by hiding any nervousness she herself may feel about leaving him. Under no circumstances, of course, should the child be forced to remain in the school if he is obviously frightened and unhappy. Simply take him home matter-of-factly without making the departure a big issue. Both you and he can return the next day for another try. It isn't unusual for a child to require a few days to get accustomed to the situation and to know for sure he's going to be picked up when school is over.

### DAY-CARE—WHERE?

Brief hours spent at nursery school can be wonderfully rewarding for a young child, but the half-day schedule obviously cannot answer the needs of a full-time working mother. Who takes over for the balance of the day—or when the child is sick and has to skip a day or two? One solution, of course, is a good substitute—whether housekeeper, friend, or relative. On the other hand, when a longer day for the child is in order, many women are anxious to find a day-care center.

If a good three-hour nursery school program seems hard to find, a day-care program for children whose mothers work full-time often seems scarcer. Despite the fact that day nurseries for the children of working mothers are standard community services in many other civilized countries—Sweden is a notable example—such services are relatively scant in the United States.

The problem of good day-care programs for preschoolers and after-school centers for their older brothers and sisters is receiving increasing community attention here, though. In a few places, church groups have led the way by establishing centers for children

of their members as well as others in the neighborhood. Obviously much more needs to be done. There
are no quick and easy solutions for this pressing problem, but all who are concerned with the healthy development of children must address themselves to it.

The President's Commission on the Status of
Women in its 1963 report "American Women" notes:

> If the family is to continue to be the core insti-
> tution of society as it has been for many centuries,
> new and expanded community services are neces-
> sary. Women can do a far more effective job as
> mothers and homemakers when communities pro-
> vide appropriate resources and when they know
> how to use such resources for health, education,
> safety, recreation, child care, and counseling . . .
>
> Child care facilities are essential for women
> in many different circumstances, whether they
> work outside the home or not. . . . The gross in-
> adequacy of present child care facilities is ap-
> parent. Across the country, licensed day care is
> available to some 185,000 children only. . . .
> Localities should institute after-school and vaca-
> tion activities, in properly supervised places, for
> school-age children whose mothers must be away
> from home during hours when children are not
> in school.
>
> Failure to assure such services reflects pri-
> marily a lack of community awareness of the
> realities of modern life. Recent Federal legisla-
> tion offering assistance to communities establish-

ing day care\* is a first step in raising its provisions
to the level of national policy. As a number of
localities have discovered, child care can be provided in many ways as long as proper standards
are assured: cooperatively by groups of parents,
by public or private agencies with fees on a sliding scale according to ability to pay; or as a public
undertaking.

The following excerpt from the report of the
President's Commission may provide an incentive to
many working mothers to take pen in hand for a note
to their Congressman:

> Since passage of the Revenue Act of 1954, the
> financing of child care by working mothers has
> been aided by the allowance of deduction from
> Federal income tax liability to help cover care of
> children and disabled dependents of women
> workers. Such deductions have been available to
> couples with the joint income of man and wife
> not exceeding $5,100 a year.
>   Advantage from this act still accrues to some
> families of moderate income and to low-income
> families, but the limit above which deductions are
> not allowed has become unrealistic. In 1954, the
> median income of families with husband working
> and wife in the labor force was approximately

---

\* In 1962 amendments to the Social Security Act earmarked
Federal funds for day-care services. These funds provided an impetus for more adequate provision of such services.

$5,336; by 1961, it has risen to $7,188. The majority of working couples are therefore ineligible for deductions.

In calculating tax deductions for child care, moreover, no account has been taken of the number of children that must be cared for.

Tax deductions for child care expenses of working mothers should be kept commensurate with the median income of couples when both husband and wife are engaged in substantial employment. The present limitation on their joint income, above which deductions are not allowable, should be raised. Additional deductions, of lesser amounts, should be allowed for children beyond the first. The 11-year age limit for child care deductions should be raised.*

## EXTRA-CURRICULAR ACTIVITIES

It's a lucky mother—and child—who can find well-planned and supervised after-school activities in their community. Such programs may be sponsored by local Y's or other youth organizations, by community centers, or by the school system itself. They may offer opportunity for sports, arts and crafts, group discussion. They are not designed to "baby-sit" for the

---

* It was raised to 12 years in the 1964 tax revision and the maximum deduction for child care was raised from $600 to $700, but only if two or more children are being cared for.

youngsters, but rather to give young people a change of pace from the classroom.

In the elementary school years, most children are interested in becoming skillful at games and in such useful household activities as cooking and minor repair jobs. They also enjoy trips—excursions to factories, museums, zoos, and aquariums give youngsters an opportunity to combine an outing with an educational experience.

Outdoor activities as well as indoor ones need the supervision of trained personnel. Staff members of day-care centers also direct sessions of listening to music, reading aloud, dramatics, and dancing. Places where a child can be alone to do homework, practice a musical instrument, or just rest should also be available.

### UP TO ALL OF US

Clearly, all the problems of working mothers and their children are not going to be magically solved by more voluntary and governmental community services. Provision for child care remains primarily the responsibility of the family, and most Americans would not want it any other way. But although we accept the premise that the family is our basic social institution and bears the chief responsibility for the well-being of its members, we must also acknowledge that all progressive countries have found it necessary to bolster the efforts of individual families.

Public nursery school education, after-school programs, day-care provisions—all cost money. Yet, nearly every child could benefit from these services, not just those whose mothers are working. Working mothers alone cannot bring about all the necessary improvements, although their families' needs may give impetus to progress. But it is going to take a lot more interest on the part of a lot more parents. The extent to which the people of the United States are willing to face and meet the needs of all children depends on their willingness, as community members, to pay the necessary price in money, time, and effort.

# 5

## THE DROP-OUT PROBLEM

NOT ALL DROP-OUTS are disenchanted teenagers. Over lunch with her friend Joyce Hickman, Trudy McKenna confessed that she had come to town to interview housekeepers. "I'm hunting for a helper," she told Joyce, "because I'm starting college next month—after all these years!"

Joyce shared her friend's excitement, and even guessed what Trudy intended to study: elementary education. Among their friends Trudy was known as The Befriender of All Children—rude, rich, or ragtaggle. Her own children were aged 12, 7 and 5. She was 37.

"Do you think you'll find it hard getting back to

the books?" asked Joyce. "When did you graduate from high school?"

"I have to confess I never did," Trudy told her. "I had to leave school when my father died. I got a job and never bothered to go back for a diploma. Last month I took some qualifying tests at our high school, and, for the record, my diploma is dated this year. There's a funny story about getting it. Do you remember meeting Barbara Johnson, who lives across the street from Harry and me?"

Joyce recalled Barbara as the wife of a somewhat stuffy bank vice president.

"Yes, that's the one. Well, her son is graduating this year and she and her husband are going to be chaperones at the senior prom. She asked us if we'd like to serve on the committee with them. I said 'no' because it just didn't seem the thing to do—after all, it's *my* graduating class, too." The two friends laughed.

Trudy's case is unusual. Not many mothers could embark on such a long-range academic program knowing they would not graduate until sometime after they reached forty. Nonetheless, Trudy will find many women her own age on campus, mothers who are enrolled for refresher courses in their particular fields. They are seeking to realize their own ambitions, searching for a fuller way to contribute to the world their children are entering.

## AT LOOSE ENDS

More and more women are realizing that they must
find ways—either in or out of the home—to do work
which they consider satisfying, useful, and worthwhile. Only then will they be at peace with themselves
and continue to grow as whole human beings. Discontented wives mean discontented husbands and
discontented children.

Modern woman finds herself in a kind of "neither-
nor" state through a myriad of developments that no
one would want to turn the clock back on, but which
also serve to leave her without the clear purpose and
sense of identity her grandmother knew. While marriage and motherhood are still a woman's main goals,
her home is clearly no longer the hive of distaff activity it once was. The fantastic recent progress in
public health and technology, which have combined
to raise living standards, prolong lives, and produce
hundreds of labor-saving devices, have so altered the
shape and form of women's lives that they can now
easily add other roles to that of mother and homemaker. Yet too many women reach their thirties before
discovering with a shock that while they lead lives
that are no longer full, they are not prepared to take
on anything else. Having devoted all their energies to
homemaking and child care, they find themselves at
loose ends when their youngsters no longer need them
full-time. Feeling discontented and disappointed

("half-used," according to some) many wish they had somehow been able to go on with the interests they had developed before their marriage.

### TWENTY EXTRA YEARS OF LIFE

Since these feelings of dissatisfaction are not unique, you owe it to yourself to sit back and think seriously about the shape and direction you want the rest of your life to take. And it is a good idea to do so whatever your own situation is at the moment—about-to-be-married, or just-married and planning a family, or married awhile with youngsters in school, or older-married with children grown. You have on the average nearly *twenty more years of life* than was common in your grandmother's day. Think of it this way: the average young woman today has about *four decades* still ahead of her by the time her last child is ready for first grade. At just a shade over thirty, obviously still active, healthy, and vigorous, she no longer even has children to look after most of the day. If she devotes herself exclusively to homemaking without giving serious thought to the world outside (a dubious practice if she is to be an interesting wife and an effective mother), she will surely find herself with a lot of "left-over life to kill" if she has not all along been doing something that gives her a continuing sense of purpose and fulfillment. A woman who in her twenties and thirties limits her interests to the nursery and the kitchen is going to find herself even more unprepared to lead a purposeful life in her forties, fifties, sixties, and seventies. And to feel like an essential part of society (which is, after all, what a purposeful life involves) women must contribute in some capacity.

## GETTING YOUR PROFESSIONAL SECOND WIND

Too many middle-aged women who earlier in life abandoned their education or careers or outside activities find themselves frustrated and angry now that they are not as needed as they once were. With less to do at home, they feel their potential is being wasted. And so it is. "We're dragging behind the rest of the world in the use of womanpower," says anthropologist Margaret Mead. Today trained women are needed in all skilled fields. "Their professional second-winds," Dr. Mead adds, "are as vital as their right to vote."

Mrs. Roberts, at forty-three, has been married nineteen years; her two sons are both in high school. A college graduate, she worked for two years as a hospital dietitian before marrying. She has time on her hands now but finds she cannot go back to her career, after such a long hiatus, without some further training, and in her community it is hard to come by.

Heeding the appeals from thousands of mature women like Mrs. Roberts, for whom the role of housewife is no longer enough, educators all over the country are engaged in planning programs of sustained or continuing education. Many colleges are now making their facilities available for those who want to renew their interrupted undergraduate study as well as for those interested in doing graduate work. Some educational institutions give counseling services only, while many others, among them Sarah Lawrence, Radcliffe, the University of Minnesota, and Brooklyn College, offer flexible courses of study specifically designed for mature women. Valuable and necessary as these programs are, they cannot begin to fill the enormous need that exists. And the usefulness of such programs is necessarily limited to a relatively small percentage of women. For too many they come too late.

### VOYAGE OF DISCOVERY

Beginning much sooner, girls should be encouraged to develop their abilities with the intention of using them later on. Early in high school, they need to receive more realistic counseling about what lies ahead for them. Parents, teachers, and others have an obligation to give girls a preview of the patterns most women's lives generally follow. All who guide the young must search for fresh ways to stimulate their thinking, enlarge their interests, and prepare them for lives that bear some relationship to the times in which they live. Surely there must be better methods than have yet been devised to help girls (many of whom stand with their right hand outstretched to receive a diploma and their left reaching out for a wedding band) to gain a sense of perspective about the lives they are likely to lead.

Most of the counseling, for example, now offered high school girls is very nearly the same as that given boys, notwithstanding the fact that the patterns of their lives are vastly different. Girls should be helped to see a preview of the life-span ahead of them once child-rearing is over. They should be forewarned about (and thus, hopefully, fore-armed against) the rusting of skills, the atrophy of abilities.

Perhaps this preview would help to capture a girl's commitment, obviously not at this period of her life to a specific vocation, but to education and training. It could encourage her to discover where her interests and abilities lie and to develop them. At the very least she could be shown a path ahead to follow if she chooses to—a path that does not renounce either the rewards of marriage and parenthood, or the enrichment of the life beyond it.

While this is not the place for a prolonged discussion of school curricula, the following remarks of educator Harold Taylor are relevant:

> A curriculum of education for our daughters must contain those studies to which they may convert their talents and their lives to the service of others and to the preservation of human values. This is not to exclude mathematics, poetry, the arts, or

history, but it is to provide an education which is liberal and vocational at the same time, since none of us can be truly liberal without knowing how to do something useful for other people. None of us can be truly vocational—that is to say—none of us can enter a calling unless he has a sense of his own identity and a full sense of what it means to be human.

But it is unrealistic to think that "a full sense of what it means to be human" can be conveyed by school people alone, or even by school counselors, assuming there were enough of them and that they all did a superb job. They can play an effective role but their efforts need re-enforcing. Community and church leaders, PTA's, Y's, and similar organizations must reach girls and help guide them. Moreover, what these influential community people do and say can modify the social climate. They can make it easier for a girl to plan a style of life that will use her energies and capabilities effectively in the home and in the world outside as well.

Importantly, the goals and aspirations of parents are not lost on their children. What a mother does— how she spends her time—influences her daughter markedly. As Dr. Bruno Bettleheim, professor in the University of Chicago's departments of psychology, psychiatry, and education has said:

> . . . the mother who urges her girl on toward
> intellectual achievement while staying at home

herself poses a contradiction which probably is not lost on the girl.

But even among mothers who have chosen to work and who love their jobs, there is a tendency to couch their reasons for working in ambiguous terms, perhaps out of a sense of misplaced guilt. In a recent article in *Daedalus*, the Journal of the American Academy of Arts and Sciences, Alice S. Rossi observed that:

> . . . a girl is seldom told that her mother works because she enjoys it or finds it very important to her own satisfaction in life, but because the money she earns will help pay for the house, a car, the daughter's clothes, dancing lessons or school tuition. In other words, working is something mothers sometimes have to do as mothers, not something mothers do as adult women. This is as misleading and distorted an image of the meaning of work as the father who tells his child he works 'to take care of mummy and you' and neglects to mention that he also works because he finds personal satisfaction in doing so, or that he is contributing to knowledge, peace or the comfort of others in the society.

There are so many ways to be a good mother that in the second half of this twentieth century there can be no justification for society's limiting women to no other commitment than an early marriage—completed by an over-sized family and under-sized aspirations.

## POSTPONING THE "I DO"

Not all girls will or should go on to college, but every girl needs as much vocational preparation as she can profitably absorb and use. H. G. Wells could easily have been thinking of the plight of today's woman when he said that "human history becomes more and more a race between education and catastrophe." High school girls who do not plan to go on to a four-year college can be encouraged to attend junior and community colleges, whose number increases yearly. Other girls, not college-bound, need to have the advantages of further training pointed out to them. The report of the President's Commission on the Status of Women reminds us that automation and economic progress are rapidly changing the job landscape. Some of the occupations that will suffer are those in which women normally find employment. Automatic data processing machines, for example, are cutting the need for bookkeepers and clerical workers. While jobs will no doubt continue to be available in these fields for some time to come, the report goes on to say, the future clearly lies with well-educated and well-trained people capable of doing professional, technical, and administrative work.

Yet today only one-half of the girls in the top third of their high school classes go on to college. And of the ablest girls who enter college, only one-third finish. Clearly it is important to urge young women to complete their undergraduate training before they marry, but understandably in our present climate, wedding bells often sound a more appealing note. To the twenty-year-old, finding a husband is often a much more attractive goal than the more remote success of a professional life. But it obviously need not be an "either-or" choice, and girls who have been given an inkling of the multiple possibilities ahead for them might find themselves able to postpone saying "I do" until after graduation.

### KEEPING A HAND IN

For those girls who do interrupt their education, more programs are needed to permit them to continue as full or part-time students when they find the time. It would help if more colleges assured those girls who leave in order to marry that they would be welcomed back in a few years. If colleges did so, many girls might take their academic work more seriously. Surely it would lessen the guilt a number of bright girls feel when they give up their career plans; it would also serve to recover much wasted talent.

At New York's Hunter College, for example, 164 fellowships, scholarships, and traineeships were awarded in 1964. About 20 per cent went to married women returning to study and professional training. The major contributor was the Federal Government, through such channels as National Defense Education Act Fellowships and awards from the National Institutes and United States Government agencies. State and city government fellowships, as well as a Hunter College Graduate Development Fund started by a small group of alumnae, are also available.

Special program arrangements can be made at Hunter for women whose home commitments prevent them from taking a full-time program. A young mother of two small children who needs a master's degree in social work (usually a two-year stint) has been permitted to stretch out her studies on a four-year basis.

When more women are encouraged to complete their education, and when it is also made easier for those who have abandoned theirs to resume it, it may well be possible to reverse the modern woman's "progression," aptly described by Columbia University's Carolyn G. Heilbrun as moving

> through diapers to the companionship of a three-year-old and the mothers of other three-year-olds, without privacy, without time to recollect herself, without time *to be*. Ahead lie unplanned years for which she has nebulous schemes. She thinks that when her children are old enough, she like MacArthur will "return." Too late she will discover that she is out of touch, out of training, and out of demand, and to be out of demand is to be excluded from the public realm where excellence is honored.

Large numbers of young women who have been to college or who have had jobs before they became mothers are eager to get out into the world again. Like their older counterparts, they too want to return to work, or resume their education, or occupy themselves with some useful and satisfying outside activity. But no matter what her age, every mother today has to create her individual design for living, and work out her own life plan. She has to take into account her special training and talents, her particular tastes and temperament, and her own unique situation.

The mother of very young children has a special problem. Busy and bogged-down as she often is, she finds it hard to see ahead, much less plan ahead. Her days are generally fairly full, and she can hardly realize that a time is coming soon when she will need something else significant to devote her energies to. But while she is still home nearly full-time, she can at least keep her hand in through continued reading, subscribing to various journals of her particular interest, attending occasional meetings, taking some courses.

Sharing experiences with women a few years ahead of them is a feature of the seminars for college-educated young mothers living within commuting distance of Cambridge, Massachusetts. The seminars have been organized by the career guidance associate at the Radcliffe Institute for Independent

Study. Through the Institute a woman with an infant, as well as thoughts about picking up the threads of a former career, is able to benefit from hearing about the experiences of a working woman with, say, a nine-year-old youngster. Obviously, not all communities can follow this pattern but endless variations of it are possible. PTA's and other groups can arrange lecture and discussion sessions for young mothers in which they can listen to professionals, compare notes, discuss career ambitions for the future, and plan ways to keep in touch with what is going on in their fields.

### EVERYBODY STANDS TO WIN

Children are better off, emotionally and intellectually, when their mothers' lives are full and satisfying. Husbands have a better time of it, too. At the very least, the dinner-table conversation is likely to be livelier when it consists of something more than a recital of household trivia. Young mothers, especially, need their husband's reassurance that their outside efforts, even though necessarily limited at first, have real value. As children get a bit older, mothers with some training—teachers, social workers, nurses, medical technicians, copywriters—find that part-time jobs keep their skills (and themselves) fully alive and ready for the challenge of full-time work, once the youngsters are relatively independent.

Mrs. Bressler, for example, who taught math before her marriage, made herself available as a substitute one day a week while her two children were young. Now that they are in school full-time, so, too, is Mrs. Bressler. They all have the same working hours and, incidentally, "new" math is no news to Mrs. B.

On the other hand, Mrs. Alexander found that working at home was best for her when the youngsters were small. An art director in her pre-mother days, she managed to round up some interesting free-lance jobs to do. But when the children were ready for school, she found herself ready for a job in a magazine office again. "I missed the stimulation of working with other people," she explained. "I get such satisfaction out of helping put the magazine out each month. Frank and the children are happier, too, now that I'm at it full-time again. "

Each woman must determine for herself how best to use the time at her disposal. But she should remember that *tempus fugit* is more than an old Roman cliché.

# 6

## RE-ENTRY DOESN'T HAVE
## TO BE ROUGH

RE-ENTERING the earth's atmosphere after a flight into outer space has its problems, but to some women they can seem child's play compared with a mother's attempt to re-enter the "labor market." Too many women complain—without having made one phone call or written a single letter—that "nobody wants an employee who is the mother of three children."

It is perfectly true that most companies are leery of hiring a young mother unless she can offer them assurance of adequate child care at home; no employer wants a worker who is absent every time her child has a cold. And *some* employers are awfully hard to convince on this score. But obviously, the

better case you can present, the better your own
chances are. (Just as obviously, the more training you
have for the job, the easier it is to dispel skepticism
about hiring you.)

### THE PART-TIME DIP—
### BEFORE THE FULL-TIME PLUNGE

Jobs with flexible working hours that permit a mother
to fulfill dual responsibilities are not as common in
the United States as they are in many other parts
of the world, but there is a definite trend toward
them. And, according to the Women's Bureau of the
Labor Department, part-time opportunities for mothers are increasing all the time.

Dipping a toe into job waters as a part-time employee can give a mother the feel of things without
disrupting her home responsibilities. After getting
into a routine of working away from home, many
women find they make the eventual transition to
full-time more smoothly than if they had plunged
right in at the beginning. Another virtue of the part-
time job is that once you are inside an organization,
you are there to be thought of if a full-time job comes
up and you are prepared for it. And you are there
to know about it if a job emerges that may suit you
but which you had not previously considered.

Mention any job being done by a woman working full-time and there is a good chance that some-

one else is doing a similar one part-time. Often it turns out to be the applicant herself who worked out the idea and the arrangements. Jane Plummer who now works part-time for an art museum in a mid-western city is a good example. Her husband was transferred there recently and Jane, an art historian, wanted to continue the work she had begun back home in the East. She outlined an interesting plan and presented it to the city arts commission. The small museum could not afford a full-time person with Jane's quali-fications, but they were more than happy to listen to her suggestion that they hire her for Tuesdays and Fridays. Since Jane has three school-age children, the two-days-a-week arrangement meets her needs perfectly.

### WHO NEEDS TO BE GREAT?

Earlier we spoke of a new form of snobbery that seems to be growing more popular lately in much of the argument about working mothers. "If they're not creative, they're not worth talking about," the feeling seems to be in some quarters. Nothing could be more absurd. You don't have to be "creative" to want to do work you consider useful and satisfying. Take Mrs. Gordon Shore, for example. Before her marriage she was a receptionist; she loved meeting people and she was good at it. Now twenty-eight, she and her husband and two youngsters live in a five-room apartment in the city. "There's just so much housework you can do in an apartment without wearing it out," she told us. "When my old firm asked me to come back four mornings a week, I jumped at the chance. My hours are the same as the children's school schedule, and Gordon's mother baby-sits if I need her to. I can't tell you the difference my working has made for all of us. Helping people, mingling with the public, talking with other adults makes me feel alive again. And, incidentally, I'm contributing more than just a little to the boys' college fund."

Another mother, Mrs. Mike Deacy, had been a secretary before her marriage. With time on her hands, and babies no longer on her lap, she decided to sharpen her skills. Whenever the opportunity presented itself during the day she turned on the radio, got out her steno book, and began taking notes. Soon she was able to keep up with the announcer well enough to warrant applying for a part-time position. She got in touch with a temporary-help agency and was offered a job immediately. She has since worked in five different offices at a regular hourly rate.

"The arrangement is a wonderful one for me since it's so flexible," Mrs. Deacy reported. "I can set my own time, which means I can be with the children after school and during vacations—in fact, whenever something comes up that requires my presence at home. Both Mike and I wish I'd thought of doing it sooner."

## MEDICINE AND MOTHERHOOD

Margot Joyce, M.D. It was a proud day when she was awarded that degree. By the time she had finished her residency, Margot was also Mrs. Jeffrey Hart, with Jeff Jr. on the way. What a shame, everyone said, never really to put that medical education to work. As she recalled it for us: "Instead of congratulations I actually received commiserations from several friends. Their reactions went from: 'Oh what a pity —after all the years you spent getting your degree!' to 'Too bad, just as you were ready to go into practice.' I found myself in the ridiculous position of almost apologizing for having had a baby, even though my husband and I were delighted."

But Margot found that in a very short time she *could* put her medical education and training back to work. She applied to the local health department, which needed physicians to staff its well-baby clinics on a per-session basis, four hours a day, three days a week. A part-time housekeeper-nurse looked after Jeff Jr. When he entered nursery school, Dr. Hart felt free to extend her working hours. She was quickly assigned more clinic sessions. Her future plans? "Jeff

Jr. is now in the first grade," she told us, "and I'm
planning to join a group medical practice here in
town on a full-time basis. Which just goes to prove
that you don't have to sacrifice your career for your
family—or vice-versa—and having both is great."

## THE SPLIT-LEVEL TRAP

Mrs. Peter Devlin, a suburban housewife with three
children of 6, 8, and 10, who recently "returned" to
writing copy for a well-known advertising agency,
had this to say: "Unless you're a victim of the split-
level trap you can't begin to appreciate how monoto-
nous life in the suburbs can be. At least it was for me.
I would find myself thumbing through magazines,
critically appraising the ad copy. I didn't realize how
obvious I was until one evening my husband said:
'If you miss it so much, why don't you take another
whack at it?' Right off, I marshaled all the reasons
why it would be impractical although actually I
knew it was exactly what I wanted to do.

"Who would care for the children? What about
the garden? Too much time would be spent commuting, etc., etc. My arguments, though advanced
half-heartedly, were enough to convince my husband
that I shouldn't try to go back, and with a flick of the
evening newspaper, he dismissed the whole idea.

"But *I* didn't. The next day I called my former

employer and discussed the possibility of my writing at home. At first he was hesitant, but on the basis of past performance he agreed to give it a try.

"Of course I realize that my case is not typical. I'm fortunate to be able to work at home, but I'm on the scene again, so to speak, and I've never been happier. I feel like a complete human being once more."

Mrs. Devlin is right, of course. Most women cannot perform their jobs at home, but each employee-mother we interviewed had managed to work out her own individual formula successfully. For Ellen Storey, going back to teaching was the right answer. Gloria Allison moved from part-time library work to full-time after a year. With no trouble at all, Marge Graham stepped back into her old job as a department store buyer. Gloria Fielding organized a catering service. The social work agency was as delighted to see Martha Melton return as she was to go back. The one thing all these women had in common was a deep sense of responsibility—both to their families and to themselves.

Sue Talbert had a harder time finding out what she wanted to do. With three children in high school and most of the day at her disposal, she never seemed to "get a thing done." Her restlessness worried the family; she had always been filled with a kind of quick energy that had led her into spurts of activity. For a time Sue attended a guitar class; luckily the guitar was only rented because she never played once the sessions ended. She took up bridge, but her husband wasn't interested so she dropped that, too. When she learned how to weave, the first item she made won first prize at the local crafts exhibit, but it was also the last piece of weaving she ever did.

One day a friend mentioned that a new organization in town was offering vocational guidance to women in just such situations as Sue's. Geared to helping mothers find part-time jobs, the service provided workshops and retraining programs and suggested potential employers. It was just what Sue needed. Before long, her natural creative bent and ability found an outlet with a firm that designed background effects for television. The discipline she'd lacked before was controlled by rigid deadlines, while the flexibility of the projects provided the variety she sought.

## NOT JUST ANY JOB WILL DO

There are ways and means of finding a job that can be ferreted out.* But obviously, not just any job will do. You want one that interests you and uses your capacities well. It may take some trial and error to find, but it will be worth it in the long run.

If you are lucky enough to have been involved

---

* If you want to start out part-time, an excellent book to help you begin digging is Joseph F. Cooper's *A Woman's Guide to Part-Time Jobs.* (Doubleday, 1963)

in work that you hoped to continue after marriage, then keeping in touch with former co-workers will often lead you directly to a job. Taking courses? Professors can often give you a lead to something suitable. If you have a profession, you very likely have retained membership in your particular organization and receive regular publications which may list job opportunities; keeping up subscriptions will keep you in touch with what is going on.

But if direct methods aren't fruitful, the answer might be to accept a job in a related field, or in another department. Helen Henderson wanted to work in the public relations department of a large industrial firm. First, she took a job as a researcher in the company's library, willing to bide her time until the job she had her sights on turned up. Her patience paid off—the opening eventually materialized.

## HOW EMPLOYERS FEEL ABOUT WORKING MOTHERS

In a recent sampling of employers, many of them called working mothers "stable," "mature," "steady," "dependable." Asked: "What would be the advantages to your business (or profession) of employing mothers?" they answered: "An organization like ours needs a cross-section of the community for both the individual and the collective good"; "Mothers have an excellent understanding of people"; "They are men-

tally adapted to meeting and serving others' needs";
"I wish there were more mothers applying—their
maturity is hard to come by, and we need it."

What about the tie to—or pull from—home? Does
it have a disrupting effect on office routine? The manager of a machine manufacturing company had a
ready answer: "Industry must be more flexible in
order to accommodate the needs of mothers to our
ranks. We must realize that there will be emergencies
that arise at home, problems to resolve, that will
necessitate phone calls during the day. There is no
reason why an employee should feel guilty simply
because a necessary phone call comes through. Our
own experience has been that a telephone call at a
fixed hour each day, say about three o'clock, has a
reassuring effect on the children and gives the mother
peace of mind. We encourage this as long as the practice is not abused. If the call is kept short and used
for touching base with the children, not random
chatting, we go along gladly."

#### "THEY ARE RESPONSIBLE—"

An owner of a real estate agency, asked how he felt
about the question of home responsibilities conflicting
with office work, replied: "The very fact that these
mothers are deeply aware of their responsibility is a
plus. Responsibility is not something that one turns
on or off at will. The employee who is conscientious

about her family will be equally conscientious about her office work and give a full day's value for her salary."

## "AND UNDERSTANDING—"

The principal of a junior high school noted that about thirty-five per cent of his faculty were mothers. Most of them had originally given up teaching to raise families, but when their own children reached school age, they felt free to return. "Our teaching mothers are highly successful," the principal said. "They're very understanding. Their first-hand experience with youngsters of their own is a big asset. And, of course, unlike women in most other professions, their 'working hours' are about the same as their children's. That automatically solves a major problem."

## "AND EFFECTIVE—"

The personnel manager of a large department store reported: "Our experience with working mothers has been excellent. Despite home responsibilities, their attendance records are generally much better than the younger female employees. We have found them especially effective as personnel interviewers—applicants respond more easily to a mature interviewer."

## "AND INDISPENSABLE—"

The director of a social agency in an eastern city admitted frankly that it would be impossible for his organization to carry the work load without the help of working mothers. He told us: "In our field, perhaps more than any other, the volume of cases has increased tremendously over the past few years. Unfortunately, the number of skilled caseworkers has not kept pace with the demand. As a result, we would be completely snowed under if we were not able to rely on the many mothers who have had social work training and experience. They are absolutely indispensable to us—as a matter of fact, our personnel policy now provides a one-year maternity leave of absence for employees who have been with us for two years. This works out well for the agency, for our clients, and for our staff."

## "—AND YET—"

While many business executives reported favorably on their experiences in employing mothers, on a full- or part-time basis, others showed some reluctance even in hiring them, much less promoting them. Their prejudice seemed more against women in general than against mothers in particular.

Although the latest census figures reveal that

there are some women in each of the 479 individual occupations listed, that hardly means that they are welcomed in all. Surveying about 2000 firms, the National Office Managers Association found that sixty-five per cent of those answering had serious reservations about women in supervisory positions. Some were certain that men would resent working for a woman, no matter how capable she was. Others explained that with a woman boss, men would chafe against the need to watch their language and tone down their behavior. And in a fair number of organizations, women are denied advancement because their employers consider them "too emotional." Emotion, of course, encompasses a wide range of expression—and no survey exists to indicate that there are more women who weep than there are men who blow their tops. Or that they do it any more often.

Perhaps a time is not too far off when the Help Wanted ads will be less rigidly divided by sex—when skill and talent alone will be the deciding factors. If we are not to continue wasting our human resources, new opportunities in fields hitherto staked out For Men Only must be opened to qualified women. From Mrs. Esther Peterson, Assistant Secretary of Labor and Special Assistant to the President on Consumer Affairs, comes the following pertinent anecdote:

Not long ago I was talking to the head of an employment service in the Midwest. "I think

you'll enjoy this story, Mrs. Peterson," he began.
"A local firm requested an engineer with some
extraordinary qualifications. We went through our
files. The only engineer who met the specifications
was a woman. We called the personnel head and
told him we had an engineer who met his needs.

" 'Send him over,' he said.

" 'It isn't a *he*. This engineer is a woman.'
There was a long pause, followed by an *oh*.

" 'Do you want us to send her over?'

"Another pause, then: 'All right, send her
over but I don't think it will work.'

"The engineer got the job, and she's been
promoted twice. I think *that* personnel man has a
new perspective on the possibilities of women
employees."

New perspectives lie ahead for us all. New challenges, too. Challenges for women to use their capacities fully. Challenges to employers to give them
equal opportunities in hiring, training, and promo-
tion. Challenges to society to learn to accept and, indeed, to welcome change so that, as the late President
Kennedy once put it, "women are used as effectively
as they can be to provide a better life for our people
—in addition to meeting their primary responsibility,
which is in the home."

# 7

## LEADING YOUR DOUBLE LIFE

PLANNING, and master-minding, organizing and managing, are key terms in the lexicon of a successful working mother. For taking on an outside job does not mean relinquishing all the inside work. And no matter how much help you get from the family itself or from a paid helper, the seemingly minor items which add up to the certain importance of a family's day-to-day well-being still depend on you.

Still, the widespread assumption that it takes a Superwoman to combine child-rearing with work outside the home requires careful examination. It is possible that this supposition is a subtle form of anti-Working Mother propaganda. No one would suggest that the job-home combination is easy, but for many mothers the satisfactions of the dual role far outweigh its difficulties. Obviously, some activities have to be curtailed when a mother goes out to work. Perhaps it's golf. Or gardening. Or bridge sessions. But it is much easier to return to this sort of thing later than it is to resume a career that has been shelved too long.

Every woman with an outside job knows that good management both at home and at work means less rush and more leisure. A working mother has more people to consider in her plan of action. Naturally the family comes first in her thoughts. And so, in the beginning at any rate, the details of each day require meticulous mapping-out to meet *everybody's* wants. After the initial back-to-work adjustment, all this blueprinting becomes less structured. Life assumes a different but natural rhythm, in tune with the needs of the whole family.

### SHARE-THE-WORK-PLAN

Lots of young married couples, when both husband and wife work, start right off by sharing domestic chores. Later on, when a baby arrives and the mother stays at home, the major part of the housework as well as the baby's care naturally becomes her province, though most young fathers do not mind helping out now and then. They pitch in whenever it is necessary, even though their wives do not have outside jobs.

Minus any old-fashioned, conflicting notions of what constitutes man's or woman's work, today's young couples usually manage to work things out domestically when the wife is ready to return to a job.

Yet even the most cooperative husband cannot be expected to take on extra household duties that interfere with his work-and-rest schedule. One man may actually enjoy helping out with cooking or marketing, but another will feel completely out of character if cast in such a role. For him, dropping the children off at school or reading to them while mother tidies up is quite enough.

In households where both parents work, fathers usually expect to take *some* part, so that child-rearing and home-management become a truly cooperative production instead of a one-woman, star-performance. Husband and wife feel closer and enjoy their youngsters more when the children are truly the concern of both. There's no doubt that the children thrive on this sense of partnership, getting, as they do, their fair share of fathering *and* mothering.

### DON'T LEAVE OUT THE CHILDREN

They usually like to help when they know their efforts are truly appreciated. If the youngsters are old enough to lend a hand with some of the housework—well and good. Certainly there's no need to dream up chores

for them, under the guise of "character-building!"
Useful work is ready and waiting.

Even a young child can handle a few such special
assignments as setting the table, dusting furniture,
shelving toys. Older children can be expected to keep
their own rooms in order—do some of the marketing
and errands and occasionally be in charge of the
smaller ones. Naturally you will not assign so many
tasks that there's no time left for fun. Every child
needs freedom to play—time to be with his friends,
or develop a hobby, or just do nothing now and then.
If not imposed upon, children take pride in helping
out at home. And the household runs more smoothly
when each member does his appropriate share of the
work.

Some families arrive at this share-the-work plan
through a "family conference" that decides what
everybody's jobs will be. Members of such a household, having a say in what can and should be done,
learn to share the responsibilities as well as the
pleasures of family life. More family-centered than
child-centered, this cooperative arrangement defers
less to the child and expects a larger, but not unreasonable, contribution from him. There is scant room
for queen bees or kingpins in a family where each
member is respected as an individual, but who nevertheless learns to give as well as get.

Children actually stand a better chance of developing a genuine sense of maturity when Mother is not always on duty to serve them. Their acceptance of reasonable responsibility for certain tasks can be a strengthening factor in their growing up. The co-operation, the family unity, the gradual independence which the youngsters experience are immeasurably valuable in their development as well-adjusted members of society. Probably more than most, a working mother keeps eyes open for household cooperation. And who knows . . . tasks that are not taken utterly for granted may well take on a shade more significance for all concerned.

## GETTING RID OF RUSH

Starting the day efficiently, with a few minutes to spare for friendly goodbyes instead of frantic reminders to "hurry up," is morale-boosting for the whole family. Morning (or evening) rush hours only create a hectic home atmosphere. Most working mothers find that work- and school-day mornings move along without a hitch when everything is ready and in order the night before—with everyone cooperating to see that clothing is ready to be put on, shoes shined, lunches packed, school books gathered and ready to be picked up. Other preparations, such as setting the breakfast table the night before, also save precious minutes in the morning.

After work, you need the leisure to listen to, talk with, and enjoy your children, without having to dive right into a multitude of household tasks. Some women manage this by sitting down with the children to relax with them for a few minutes before starting dinner. Others let the youngsters help with dinner preparations, chatting the while. If you have a house-keeper who prepares the evening meal—or at least gets things started for you—kitchen-concentration is one item you can cheerfully check off your agenda.

The attention you give to the youngsters' home-work when they need your help, or the few minutes you spend admiring a good arithmetic paper or a painting done at school—or just listening and talking about the day's happenings—mean a great deal. To be able to give this time, working mothers establish their own priorities. Unless you have full-time help, you'll probably not put extra scrupulous housecleaning at the top of your "must" list.

### TIME OUT FOR TREATS

As a job-holder, you'll find yourself planning occasions to be with the children—to be attentive to their needs and to enjoy their companionship without per-mitting dozens of workaday details to intrude. You may set aside a Saturday or Sunday for special out-ings—a trip to the beach, a visit to a museum, a family picnic. It might surprise you to realize that you are spending more time having fun with your children than many stay-at-home mothers.

This does not mean that you should plan every single free moment with the children. There are times when you and your husband need to get away together—and times, too, when you owe yourself a few purely personal hours. It isn't selfish to allot time to yourself and your husband minus the rest of the clan. A husband and wife need leisure together apart from the children, just as much as the children need to be away from them. A marriage choice is made, after all, because two people want to be with each other. The choice becomes pointless if there is never any time to be alone together. Remember that as youngsters grow beyond their baby years, they have outside interests as well as friends of their own and obviously do not need (or even want) you with them every minute you can be.

Opportunities for the whole family to be together always present themselves in the natural course of events. The children can go along with you when you do the Saturday marketing—a kind of family outing in itself. Youngsters usually enjoy supermarkets and shopping centers and like to be consulted on family purchases.

### PRACTICAL POINTERS

Going to work seldom becomes such a huge production that you have to fortify yourself with 1001 time-saving tips. And time-savers that work out well for one working woman will not necessarily find your schedule a comfortable fit. But it does help to know something about how other mothers are managing and to compare notes on housekeeping shortcuts. Some ideas, gleaned from experience, are applicable to every working mother. New and better ways of handling your own responsibilities will come to you as your ingenuity encounters experience.

Have you tried a written schedule? Right at the start, you might make things easier by writing down everything that has to be done, and then figuring out the best time for doing it. You may find yourself radically altering some of the routines you have always been used to. While you are not planning to run your house on a precise timetable, just putting your plan on paper will give you an idea of the scope of your job. It may even help you to cut and prune the nonessentials. (If the whole *idea* of lists depresses you, start one headed "Make list." When you've finished writing down chores to be done, scratch the first item as taken care of—the feeling of accomplishment will last as long as you can postpone reality.)

Planning your menus for the entire week (whether you have a housekeeper or not) eliminates last-minute decisions and harried shopping expeditions. Do your main marketing once a week. Stock up on staples, canned and frozen goods, and then fill in with fresh fruits, vegetables and meat as needed during the week. Plenty of freezer storage space is a boon to busy shoppers.

Quick-fix meals can be as nutritious and appetizing as those that require a lot of time and effort. If you do all your own cooking, you can save time by serving course-in-one meals frequently—casseroles, hearty salads, soups that combine meat or fish, and stews that defy your family's identifying abilities—but go down as fast as the guessing goes on.

Lists should be kept in strategic places. A pad and pencil somewhere near the refrigerator make it possible for you to jot down needed items as you think of them. A bulletin board in your kitchen makes a fine place not only for reminders but notes and family communications as well. It also provides a convenient spot for posting special chores to be done by the youngsters, and for tacking up menus and schedules of the children's outside activities. Even though she has instructed her substitute, a mother likes to leave messages for the family that bear her personal touch and show her always-present interest—"Cookies are for snacks, honey, but the pie is for dinner." Or "Stevie—remember to take permission slip for school outing." The family bulletin board can serve, too, as a place for youngsters to tack up their own messages, as well as special school papers and school announcements.

Paper and plastic are great labor-savers. Attractive plastic mats and table covers, paper napkins, paper towels—all cut down on everyday laundry. During summer months, some women use plastic-coated paper plates and cups several times a week to save on dishwashing. Used for cold dishes and picnic meals, the plastic substitutes can be festive. But when you must wash dishes, rinse them with hot water and let them dry in the rack. A dishwasher, of course, is a fine convenience, especially for a large family.

To help young children learn to be orderly, and to make things easier on everybody, you can see that clothes-closet rods are within their reach, so that they can hang up their own things. Having their own laundry hamper might even provide an incentive for them to deposit soiled clothing, which would make it easier for you to collect washing. Finally, shoebags inside the closet nearest the house entrance for keeping caps, mittens, scarves, and rubbers that have to be found quickly on cold or rainy mornings avoid frantic scrambling and frazzled nerves.

**PUTTING YOUR PHONE TO WORK**

How much time is your telephone saving for you? Use it, whenever possible, to shop for advertised items that you do not need to inspect in the store. You could even do your main grocery marketing by phone, making arrangements with a local merchant for delivery service. Your food budget might suffer a little, but that is one of the hidden costs of working. On the other hand, some mothers justify the expense by saying that ordering by phone eliminates all the "impulse buying" they used to do at supermarkets.

Keep important telephone numbers on a pad beside your phone at home. For instance:

| | |
|---|---|
| Your office number | Fire department |
| Your husband's office number | Drug store |
| Neighbor, friend, or relative to be called in an emergency | Markets |
| Police department | Doctor |

These are posted so that your helper and your family will have them at a glance for quick reference. Your children should know that they can phone you in an emergency, and be told how to reach you. (To prevent a sudden piling up of extra charges on your telephone bill, you should explain what constitutes a "necessary" call.)

Obviously, not all working mothers pursue every detail in precisely the same way—nor would anyone want them to. But it's surprising how much time can be saved by what appear to be minor points of efficiency.

**TWO DOUBLE LIVES**

Let's have a brief look at how two quite different working mothers handle their double jobs:

Blanche Apton works part-time five mornings each week in the office of a nearby high school. Her four-year-old daughter, Suzanne, goes to nursery school from 9 A.M. to noon. The arrangement suits both Suzy and her mother remarkably well. Her daughter is getting a chance to know children her own age, and Mrs. Apton is keeping her skills from growing rusty.

Later on, when Suzy enters elementary school, Mrs. Apton intends to take a job with longer hours. In the meantime, she enjoys her work and is gaining valuable experience which is bound to stand her in good stead for the future.

At the moment, Mrs. A's daily schedule goes something like this :

| | |
|---|---|
| Early morning: | Breakfast for the family. |
| | Get Suzy ready for nursery school. |
| | Straighten up kitchen and bedrooms. |
| | Off to school and work. |
| Noon: | Home for lunch with Suzy. |
| Afternoon: | Suzy takes nap or rest period. |
| | Clean house (One room per day.) |
| | Straighten up and dust the rest. |
| | Do laundry or ironing. (The big pieces are sent out.) |

Evening:           Prepare dinner. (Joe Apton usually gets home from work at about 6 P.M., and the family has dinner together before Suzy is tucked into bed.)

One evening each week, usually on Thursday or Friday—the Aptons shop for groceries. Additional supplies are picked up as needed from day to day. By alternating jobs throughout the week—one afternoon for rinsing things out, one for pressing, one for cleaning—Mrs. Apton keeps up with the housework. And she still has plenty of time to read and to sew—and to get a kick out of her small daughter's companionship as well.

Mrs. Bernstein, on the other hand, has a full-time executive position with a large corporation and her 9 to 5 schedule gives her much less leeway. Even though her two children, Kenny, 12, and Alice, 10, are in school, someone needs to be there when they get home. Mr. and Mrs. Bernstein decided that homemaking help was a must, not only for the children but for them too. Despite the help of a full-time housekeeper, Mrs. Bernstein finds plenty of "overtime" duties awaiting her at home. Here is a look at her daily schedule:

Mornings:   Breakfast for and with the family. Everybody gets ready for work and for school. Mrs. Bernstein doesn't bother with much tidying up because her housekeeper comes in around ten and takes over. The children go to school by bus, and their father drives them to the bus stop on his way to work.

Evenings: Housekeeper fixes dinner and leaves after Mrs. B. gets home. She and the children add the finishing touches, and when Mr. B. gets in, everybody enjoys dinner together. After dishes are stacked in the dishwasher, there's time for watching TV, reading, or helping the children with homework when they need a little assistance. Mrs. B. reminds the children to see that their school clothing is conveniently ready for the next morning. If there are special instructions for the housekeeper, Mrs. B. writes a note for her and posts it on the kitchen bulletin board.

On weekends, Mrs. Bernstein outlines the week's menus. She prefers to do the marketing herself on Saturdays although her housekeeper makes some purchases during the week. Sunday is a day of relaxation for the whole family. The Bernsteins often go out to dinner on Sunday afternoons or visit with friends and relatives. Every day of the week does not necessarily follow the same pattern. Like all parents, the Bernsteins sometimes enjoy getting away by themselves, whether it's going to the theater, a concert, a party, or just to the neighborhood movies. Then, either the grandparents or a sitter stay with the children.

Even though domestic help relieves Mrs. Bernstein of many tasks, she is still the one "in charge" of home management. She helps to plan and oversee (from her office, at times) the children's after-school activities. It's up to her to manage such essentials as marketing and meal-planning, shopping for clothing and household items, in addition to the many other details that have to be handled in all households.

### WHEN HELP IS WANTING

Most mothers with full-time jobs need some domestic help. Other mothers with part-time jobs and no help manage their dual role by omitting details that might otherwise rock the family boat. Mrs. Crosby, for instance, with two youngsters in grade school, works for a nearby law firm from ten to three. This means she can see the children off to school in the morning and be home when they get back.

"Before I went back to work, I was a real fusspot around the house," Mrs. Crosby admitted. "I couldn't stand to see ashes in an ash tray, Sunday papers strewn about, anything out of place. As I look back now I must have seemed pretty ridiculous. I'd pounce on ash trays before my husband had even finished his cigar . . . wince at the slightest disorder and generally make myself a nervous wreck. Going back to work has given me a new perspective. I can resist those reflex actions to straighten up all the time —after all, things are going to be askew again in a little while. I can look at ashes in the tray without falling apart and toss the Sunday papers around with as much abandon as the rest of the family. Don't get me wrong. Going back to work hasn't made a slob of me, but it has taught me to conserve my energy for the things that matter and that give me real satisfaction."

Another experienced working mother has given us these words of advice about housework: "Don't do it all. Don't do it alone. Don't do it in the old way." Almost every woman with a double job can put this philosophy into practice. After all, the purpose of your outside work is to add a plus value to your life. If, instead, the workload saps your strength and unravels your nerves you will need to review and revamp your plans.

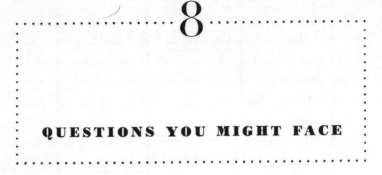

# 8

## QUESTIONS YOU MIGHT FACE

THE SCENE is familiar: the youngsters are ready for bed and company is arriving for dinner. First the guests say to the parents: "My, haven't those good-looking kids of yours grown!" Next they talk to the children. "What are you going to be when you grow up, Peter?" This month Pete hopes to collect garbage. Last month he wanted to pilot a jet. Everybody laughs.

"And Kathy, what would you like to be?"

"A mommy," answers Kathy. Everyone smiles approvingly.

The setting *is* familiar, but today the lines are changing. Within the scene's framework, new patterns of thought are preparing new patterns of behavior. Kathy's father stirs the conversational fires with another question. "Yes, Kathy, that's what you're going to *be*, but what are you going to *do?* Mommy's a mommy, but she's a chemist, too."

He wants Kathy, though she is only six, to get a beginning glimmer of the directions her life can take. He feels that it may help to break a mold that has restricted the growth of so many women in our time. And, of course, the example Kathy's mother sets is bound to have a strong influence on her. Both her mother and father hope that it may minimize for Kathy the dilemmas that confront too many of today's bright and energetic young women.

While thousands and thousands of women are managing dual roles with skill and with pleasure, they do encounter problems, too, from time to time. They will be the first to tell you that they have occasional doubts, occasional worries. Some of the questions they ask may be similar to ones you have been concerned about. And some of the answers may give you a clue to a perplexing problem of your own.

*My husband thinks it's fine for me to work, and he is glad that I enjoy my job. He helps me as much as he can with some of the household chores. But he is careful to keep this quiet among his men friends, and he wouldn't think of lending a hand when friends or relatives come to visit. He claims it's all too un-masculine.*

Many men, today, do not feel in the least bit threatened by helping out at home now and then. Others, however, have been brought up to believe strongly that housework is strictly a woman's province, and they cannot be expected to overcome such feelings overnight. The husband who helps, even against his own convictions, is probably trying to see things in a new light. Certainly he is being considerate, and his cooperation should be appreciated. But if he feels more comfortable keeping it a private concern, there's no reason not to respect his wishes.

*"What did you bring me, Mommy?" That's the instant greeting I get from my five-year-old daughter when I come home from work. That's because I started by bringing a little gift, and now it's expected. Suzy is actually angry or hurt if I forget!*

Many working mothers (and some fathers, too) get into the habit of bringing a toy or gift home occasionally as an end-of-the day surprise. Some women, who feel a twinge of guilt about working away from home, may give these gifts every day to soothe their own feelings, but it isn't advisable to make this a routine production. Appeasing a child in this way doesn't really help him at all. It is more likely just to make him greedy. An occasional surprise is fun to give and fun to get. The child who asks, "What did you bring me?" every single evening can simply be told that Mommy doesn't *always* bring presents . . . just sometimes.

*I get home from the office at around four. More often than not my housekeeper reports that John, who's eight, has been teasing the life out of his five-year-old sister. This worries me because I'm not there to settle things. He doesn't do it much when I'm home.*

Sisters and brothers of this age have little in common except their parents. They cannot be expected either to spend much time with each other or to play happily together. One good way to bring about better feelings between them is to encourage their activities away from each other. Your son is much more interested in playing with boys his own age than he is with his sister, and he should be given free rein to do so. And you'll want to invite younger children over to play with your daughter. Consider, too, that the five-year-old may provoke much of the teasing. Tell your housekeeper not to take sides or encourage the younger one to tattle. This will let them both know that they do not have to battle for her attention.

*I work three days a week, and when I come home I find that my 11-year-old boy has "forgotten" to do most of his chores. I'm tired of having to remind him constantly, and*

*I don't like to nag. What can be done to make him feel a little more responsible?*

Most youngsters around this age are naturally more taken up with their own interests than with the chores that need to be done. You stand a good chance of getting better cooperation by planning ahead with your son, and together making out a reasonable time schedule. Try not to assign chores at a time when he is busy with his own important projects, and, if possible, give him tasks not too far out of line with his interests. Children really want to be fair and cooperative. A little tact (plus some reminding) goes a long way toward helping them to become more responsible. Some mothers leave a brief list of things to be done on the family bulletin board or blackboard, and let the children check off the chores as they are done. This may be the only reminder that they need and, if the chores are "extras," a little extra money is a powerful incentive.

*Now that I'm working, my ten-year old wants her allowance raised. It's no hardship, but I don't get the point of giving her a fixed amount. She spends it on some kind of foolishness the day she gets it, and then is always after us to give her more whenever she wants something.*

There is a point in allowances, even if children don't spend their money in ways that seem wise to their parents. They can probably learn how to use money only by trial and error. If your daughter spends her allowance right away and forgets that she wanted to keep some, say, for the movies on Saturday, then she is learning something. Either she won't be able to go, or she'll feel the pinch when she has to pay you back.

Has her allowance increased as her needs have increased? Is she getting about the same amount as her friends? You can help her to budget her allowance so it will last and cover the things she wants most. But the final decision as to how to spend it must be hers if she is eventually to learn the purpose of an allowance and the value of money.

*My husband likes to help around the house—in fact, he's a better cook than I am. But what about all this sex-role perception I've been reading about? Do we need to worry that Joe Jr. will think his father is a sissy?*

Obviously, the household jobs he likes to do don't make Joe Sr. feel threatened or uncomfortable. If he isn't, Joe Jr. won't be either. There's no danger of Dad's masculinity going down the drain with the dish water.

*We're not worried because Billy, two and a half, loves to play with dolls, but Grandpa certainly is. He babysits for me the two mornings a week I work. How can we re-assure Grandpa?*

Tell Grandpa that there's no reason to be upset. At this age youngsters don't make clear-cut distinctions between boy and girl activities. That will begin to appear in a year or so. It might reassure Grandpa to know that a husky, all-American football player we know couldn't be separated from his doll when he was two.

*What's to be done when children dawdle on school mornings? My second-grader is a very slow starter. This is really aggravating when I have to keep my eye on the clock so that I don't get a late start to the office.*

Dawdling can sometimes be caused by too much prodding and too many reminders to "Hurry up." Trying to rush a child through his morning routines creates tension and resistance, besides. True, many children are somewhat slow about getting up and getting ready for school. Probably the best solution is to allow extra time, by getting up earlier and waking the child a little earlier. If he needs some help in dressing or getting ready, you can more easily give it when there's enough time allotted. Some children seem to need to be a bit lazy before they are fully awake and raring to go. Its important to make the morning as pleasant as possible and to resist the temptation to rush the children. Careful planning can start the day right.

*At first my husband and I were amused when our ten-year-old called practically everything "cool." Now almost all of his conversation is slang, a good deal of it crude. Our helper doesn't mind, but we do.*

Some slang is amusing and effective, but a steady diet of it can be irritating to parents who wonder if their own good speech habits are making any impression at all on their children. Believe it or not, they are! But parents won't realize quite how much, until their youngsters outgrow (as they do) the need to use slang constantly. Since there's little you can do to keep your son from using, and over-using, the current fads in slang, you might as well relax and not "hear" some of it. If your helper doesn't know what words you do object to, tell her. Ban the really crude ones, but don't despair—there's every reason to believe that the speech your son is accustomed to hearing from you is not lost on him and will be in evidence once he outgrows the slang age.

*My husband and I are editors, and meeting deadlines sometimes leaves us "bushed." We'd love to go away by ourselves for a weekend without our six-year-old, but I feel a little guilty about it because we both work. Our*

*daughter does beautifully, loves our housekeeper, and be-
sides, Grandma has volunteered to pitch in any time.*

Of course, you and your husband need some guilt-
free time away together by yourselves. All parents—
working or not—have a right to, as well as a need for,
some time off now and then, away from the children.
They need time together to appreciate each other as
they are, not simply as Mary's and Johnny's mother
and father. Not that they are going to forget their children or forget for a minute that they are parents, but
they need an opportunity now and then to be together
just as husband and wife.

It is fine that you have an excellent housekeeper
whom your child loves and on whom you can rely. As
for Grandma, you don't want to deprive her of the
fun of taking over on an occasional weekend. And
you don't want to deprive your daughter, either, of
the rewarding experience of getting to know Grandma
better.

*I worry about my ten-year-old daughter because she isn't
hungry in the morning. All she wants for breakfast is a
glass of milk, and I don't have the time to wait for her
to "work up" a good appetite before I leave for the office.*

Many children have difficulty eating a big breakfast before they go to school. However, this is an important meal because it supplies energy for the morn-

ing's work and play. Of course, it won't do any good
to try to force, or even to coax a child to eat when he
lacks appetite, but there are ways to help him get into
the habit of eating *something* nutritious in the morning. Remember that breakfast doesn't have to follow
a conventional pattern. The youngster who can't face
an egg in the morning might well enjoy another pro-
tein food such as cheese on toast, and a piece of fresh
fruit. In winter, some children like a breakfast of hot
soup, toast, fruit or juice, and milk. You can experi-
ment with a variety of menus—and offer *small* portions to the child who currently does not want a big
meal. The main thing is to encourage children to eat
something for breakfast so that they will not get into
the habit of neglecting this meal together. Of course,
over-all eating habits are what count in keeping a
child well-nourished. It doesn't all hinge on one meal.
A good lunch (hopefully hot) at school, plus a nutritious after-school snack and a well-planned dinner add
up to a balanced diet.

*My mother cares for my two children while I'm at the
office. For the most part, this works out well, but occasionally she and I disagree about discipline. I'd like to handle
this situation better.*

No two people discipline in exactly the same way.
Perhaps in your mother's era discipline was stricter.

It won't hurt the children to be a little neater, say, if that's what she wants. Since things go well most of the time, you and your mother should be able to discuss during the quiet moments the issues that bother you both. Understanding her point of view can go a long way toward having her accept yours. Children catch on to the fact that there are differences in what people feel are important, but they must also learn that Grandma's word goes when she is in charge. Without fussing too much about nonessential details, you can work things out without friction and without undermining Grandma's authority.

*I have two children, seven and nine. Recently I returned to work part-time; the job is interesting and I enjoy it very much. But lately I've read a few articles on "what makes a good mother," and I'm beginning to feel a little worried about being away from the children for several hours each day. I can't help thinking that there may be something unnatural about my not wanting to be home with them all the time.*

You are voicing a concern which bothers many women. Apparently the myth of the so-called perfect parent is still with us even though child-care experts have made it increasingly clear that all kinds (and quite different kinds) of people make very good parents. If it were true that every mother had to be exactly like every other mother, and do exactly the same things, there would be no room for a single spark of individuality in this world. Fortunately that's impossible because it would be far from ideal. No two children are precisely alike, nor do they all require the same brand of care and treatment from their parents. Besides, there's no reason to believe that constant proximity guarantees good mothering! As a matter of fact, studies show that when mother and child are always together they can become too dependent upon one another. It is important for children to develop good relationships with people other than their parents. A child is doing just that when he learns to rely on a good mother-helper for part of the time.

*Our ten-year-old is a terrific tomboy, wanting always to wear blue jeans and play boys' games with her brothers. She does dress up when she visits me at the office because she knows I expect it of her, but for the most part we have quite a battle about getting her into a dress. This worries her father and me, and we're not sure what to do.*

Being a tomboy at ten can be a perfectly normal phase in a girl's development, especially if she is good at sports and has older brothers to play games with. It would be useless to try to put a stop to it right now, and there's no reason to. You'll probably seen an enormous change as she nears her teens. Then she'll take an interest in feminine clothes and fripperies. And naturally, boys—though in a new way. Only rarely does this change not occur in the teens; if it *doesn't* happen, you would be wise to seek professional guidance.

*I have an opportunity to return to my job as a designer, either full or part-time, and I'd love to do it. However, this would mean entering my four-year-old in a nursery school. He's ready for it, but I'd like to make the transition easy. Are there any do's and don't's for this?*

Most children take to nursery school immediately and don't need any prolonged introductions. Other children, who are shy and need more time to adjust, do better if they are introduced to the school more slowly. If this is so with your child, you will want to stay with him, or in a room nearby (whichever the school advises), until he builds up an attachment to the teacher and to the other children that will stand him in good stead when you no longer stay at school.

Going to nursery school represents a major change in your son's life. Having you return to work is another. Asking him to face both at once is too much. You will do better to wait until your son is happy in nursery school before you accept the job. Perhaps working part-time would be best at first. Once your child makes new friends at school and enjoys the new environment, you can always switch to full-time if you want to, and if you have a good substitute to take over for you.

*Since returning to my job as research analyst a few months ago, I have noticed a change in attitude in my two daughters, age seven and nine. Although they are just as loving and affectionate as ever, they now tend to bring their problems to our housekeeper, even when I'm home. I find this transfer of allegiance very disturbing.*

Most likely your housekeeper is not aware she is assuming so much responsibility—indeed, she may not even notice that they come to her rather than to you since this is simply the normal routine of her day with the girls. The next time it happens, perhaps you could say something like this to her privately: "I'm so glad that the children love and trust you, but I enjoy helping them, too. Next time the girls come to you with a problem when I'm home, why don't you suggest that you all come to me to find out what I think?" Your children have an abundance of affection to give, and while they love you best as their mother, it is good that they can also love the woman who stands in for you.

*I am a nurse who gave up my profession after my first son was born. I now have two boys in junior high. There is an acute shortage of nurses at the local hospital, and they have been trying to prevail upon me to return. (And frankly, I'd love to.) This would present no problem as I could do so on a private-duty basis, fitting my hours to the boys' school and vacation schedules. My husband has left the decision entirely up to me. The only obstacle is my mother-in-law. Her husband died when her three children were quite small, and she was forced to work to support her family. She is now adamantly opposed to mothers working unless they have to. If I do return, my next-door neighbor can always take over if it is necessary.*

The very fact that your mother-in-law worked outside the home and yet was successful in raising her family should prove a strong point in your favor. Also, you are fortunate in having an ally in your husband. Why not suggest that he approach her? He could explain that you are reluctant to waste your years of training, that you would be performing a needed service in the community and that the children would not suffer in any way. You might both assuage her doubts by suggesting that you go back on a trial basis. Once you have returned and she realizes that you will be free to spend time with your children between cases and that they are properly taken care of during your absence, she is sure to come around, and quite likely will develop a new respect for you in the process. But in the long run, of course, the final decision is yours and your husband's.

*My nine-year-old daughter is dying to go to camp this summer, and I thought it a fine idea until my sister-in-law tried to dissuade me. She thinks that since I am away at work so much of the time, it would be wrong to deprive the child of my companionship for the entire summer. Now I'm doubtful what would be best.*

If your child wants to go to camp, there certainly is no reason to keep her at home. The fact that she isn't hesitant about being away from home actually shows how secure she feels and how sure she is of your love.

Most children, even the very youngest, spend almost all their summer freedom out-of-doors, anyhow, frequently reporting to home base only for lunch. The chances are she would be out playing most of the day even if she didn't go away. And if her friends were at camp, she may even construe your working as keeping her from a wonderful camping experience.

Camp-life can be a good, healthful experience for children. Many mothers, working or not, solve the vacation problem this way. There's an informative booklet which you might want to read: *How to Choose a Camp For Your Child* by Ernest Osborne, Pamphlet Number 231, Public Affairs, 22 East 38th Street, New York, N. Y. 10016.

*Getting my two girls to bed at night on a reasonable schedule presents my biggest after-work problem. Besides the need to talk over events of the day, get homework done, watch a little TV, decide on tomorrow's outfits, brush teeth and bathe, my children will go to any lengths simply to avoid going off to bed. How can I cut down "bedtime hubbub"?*

Even for non-working mothers, these hours are usually crammed with activity and require scheduling and organization if they are to be pleasant and relaxing ones.

A regular time for doing homework should be established, as well as a definite time for turning off the TV set. Parents who find being firm just about the most wearying part of parenthood find following the "TV rule" just about the most difficult of all—but allowing it to slip can be the biggest possible time (and mind) waster.

Decisions about clothes for the next day can best be settled at the beginning of the week. With five outfits washed and ironed and ready for wearing by Sunday night, decisions on which one to wear can be left until morning as weather and mood dictate.

# 9

## THE PRICE YOU PAY

TO THE innumerable women for whom an outside job is right, the rewards are enormous, but they do exact some cost—in time, in actual money, in emotion. So whether you have a job or are now considering one, you must be prepared to take into account "the price you pay."

Even if you are lucky enough to have the most marvelous housekeeper in the world, and a husband who does not mind pitching in now and then, the chief home responsibilities are yours. Whether you actually carry out the details or not, it is still up to you to see that Dad's dinner jacket is home from the cleaner on time, that Mary's new dress is hemmed for the birthday party, that Billy keeps his dentist appointment, that the repair man fixes the oil burner. A woman is never not-a-woman, whether she works or not.

### "FROM SUN TO SUN . . ."

"It's funny," said Martha Gilman, "but even though Charles has two secretaries, I'm the one who's expected to call up the bank if our statement looks wrong, or write a note to the magazine that's made an error in our subscription. I don't mind doing any of these extra little things, but it does amuse me to realize that even in this day and age woman's work is never done."

Attending to the millions of details involved in running a household falls to your lot, just as the burden of its support is your husband's, whether you decide to work or not. He is practically always the main breadwinner, and in any case, his is the primary and the ongoing responsibility. If your husband is too busy with his own work to give you any assistance at home, or if he just doesn't feel like it, complaining is hardly the answer, especially if you yourself have opted for an outside job. Perhaps, like Mrs. Gilman, you can be prepared to be amused. In any event, you'd better be prepared. Martyrs make poor mothers. They not only make impossible working mothers, but they make working impossible—certainly as far as the family is concerned.

The area of household responsibility classified as

"minor household emergency" is very likely the one to cause the most inconvenience to a mother who works. Emergencies can arise whether you go out to work or to a tea party, but there is a difference. A sudden rainstorm may flood the basement and ruin a basket of clean laundry waiting there for your helper to iron when she gets in. If you had been next door having coffee, you would have known that a heavy rain would be likely to overflow into the cellar, and you would certainly have raced to save the clean clothes. The extra work involved may be all you do not need to climax a day already filled with crotchety clients or unmet deadlines. But working mothers, probably even more than others, learn to take things in their stride. They catch on rather quickly to the futility (as well as the foolishness) of magnifying a minor nuisance into a major tragedy. As one successful working mother remarked, "It's not too hard to learn to roll with the punches, and most of them are minor jabs, anyway."

### TWENTY-FOUR CARAT GUILT

There's hardly a working mother who doesn't feel some guilt some of the time. Unfortunately, our society does not do much to lessen the feeling. If anything, it serves to compound the guilt some mothers feel by the very contradictory attitudes it takes. While stressing the value of everyone's reaching his (and *her*) full potential, it still does not give women sufficient help and encouragement to enable them to change their traditional role. And at the same time, it very often overemphasizes the rights and needs of children as it de-emphasizes the rights and needs of parents, thus adding fuel to the fire of conflict.

Obviously, just saying "don't feel guilty" to a mother in conflict with the demands of home and work will not automatically erase her guilt. Were guilt that easily routed, large numbers of psychiatrists would have to pack up their couches or their tranquilizers and steal quietly away to a new specialty. One researcher noted that "professional mothers tried too hard to prove to themselves and their relatives that they weren't actually neglecting their children—as a matter of fact, they spent as many actual hours with them on the average as the homemakers did." Still and all, guilt does persist and mothers who work have their job as a handy whipping boy to beat on whenever something goes wrong at home.

Take Leona Bissell, for example. One afternoon she was summoned from a City Council budget meeting by a phone call from her housekeeper. "Don't be alarmed, Mrs. Bissell. I'm in Dr. Krieger's office at the hospital. He's just finished setting Chip's collarbone. He broke it falling out of Pete Marsh's tree house. Mrs. Marsh drove us here, and she's taking us back now."

"Thanks, Ellen, I'll be right home. Let me talk to the doctor." Even though Mrs. Bissell knew there was nothing more she could have done had she been at home, she was still plagued with the feeling that *had* she been there and not at work, Chip would not have had that accident.

In truth, her son frequently played in Pete's tree house, and as her husband pointed out that evening, "the only difference is that Mrs. Marsh drove to the hospital instead of you. Suppose you didn't work, but had simply been out marketing. Nothing different would have happened. And Chip, that big ham, got an enormous kick out of telling you all about it later."

Mrs. Andrews is another case in point. She worried constantly about her daughter Lucy's "just average" grades and tended to ascribe them to the fact that she was a working mother. Otherwise, why wasn't Lucy the all-A student her older sister Emily had been at her age? (Mrs. A. wasn't working then.) The children's pediatrician reassured Mrs. Andrews on several scores. "Lucy," he reminded her, "is a social, outgoing child and already a talented ballet dancer. Just because Emily was a whiz in math and English is no sign that Lucy must be."

The doctor continued: "I can remember how impressed I was with Lucy last year when she organized that summer recreation program for the younger kids in the neighborhood. What ordinary twelve-year-old could sustain and direct an activity like that for two months? And didn't you tell me she earned enough for most of her school clothes? I'll make you a bet that Lucy's going to be happier and more successful, too, than 95 per cent of her classmates, honor students included!"

It is difficult to handle guilt—it is so pervasive and so easily accentuated. It can lead a mother to misinterpret the everyday ups and downs of childhood and blame herself and her job for what may be only normal "misbehavior." It can goad her into taking more car pools, attending more school meetings than could possibly be considered reasonable. Mothers who work have built-in receptors for guilt, but, if it is not overwhelming, they can usually reduce its intensity by airing the facts with a sympathetic listener—their husband, a friend, a fellow worker. Guilt should not have to demand as heavy a price as many working mothers pay.

### THOSE OUTSIZE ACTIVITIES

"I'll never get over what a nut I used to be," Marianne Cooper, mother of two school-age children, told us. "I worked five mornings a week window-dressing for a department store, and I loved it. But I also managed to be a Den Mother, Chairman of the PTA program committee, and Fund Raiser Extraordinary for everything from arthritis to tuberculosis. I never missed my turn in the car pool, either, and I even used to volunteer to substitute whenever another mother couldn't make it.

"It took me an awfully long time to catch on to what I was doing. I was out to prove to all those non-working mothers that I could do a better job than they could. I finally got the picture when my neighbor who doesn't work complimented me for the umpteenth time. 'You're so wonderful, Marianne,' she said, and she meant it. 'Here I am feeling guilty whenever anyone asks me what I do. And there you are—with an interesting job, two marvelously brought up kids, and *all* those other activities.'

"*All those other activities*," Mrs. Cooper went on, "was just what Phil, my husband, had been talking about for months. And imagine my stay-at-home neighbor feeling guilty. I started trimming those outsize activities to a more normal amount the very next day. And I don't mind telling you that Phil and the boys were glad I did."

Too many working mothers try to do more and be more than other mothers. That's a heavy price to pay for a job. If Mrs. Cooper's story has a familiar ring, you might do well to review your schedule and ask yourself: Are all these extracurricular activities really necessary—or am I needlessly trying to make up for the guilt I feel about being a working mother?

## EXPECTING TOO MUCH, OR TOO LITTLE, OF YOUR CHILDREN

Some mothers pay for their job-connected anxieties by never expecting anything of their children. Others react in just the opposite fashion by making excessive demands on their young. Mrs. Harley belongs in the first category. She lays out her youngsters' clothes each night, although both of them are old enough to do it themselves. Neither one is required to wash a dish or put away a book or hang up a coat. "I'd rather do it myself," says Mrs. H., "than ask June or Jim to help. They have their homework to do and their practicing —that seems enough to me."

Mrs. Karlan goes to the other extreme. On the defensive a good deal of the time, she insists that fourteen-year-old Ann do the marketing, plan all the meals, and take charge of Bobby, the eight-year-old. "Ann's going to run a household of her own some day," says Mrs. K., "and it'll do her good to learn now."

These kinds of responses are obviously unhealthy for both Mrs. Harley and Mrs. Karlan, as well as for their families. If you choose to work, you must be able to do so with some degree of assurance that it is right. Otherwise, you'll do better by everyone, including yourself, if you stay home. After all, motherhood is a delightful state, and if you have some serious and satisfying outside interests to pursue now and when the children are older, you should think twice about whether a job is for you. There are worse things than being your own boss and being able to decide for yourself what you want to spend your time on, in exactly what ways, and for how long. But you may be bored or discontented staying home. You may feel, as many mothers do, that you are not using yourself to capacity. So if your motivations for wanting an outside job are sound, then you have the right and responsibility to make a guilt-free try at a job.

This does not mean that if Sally's marks take a slump, if Mark acts unbearably rude, if Kathy has an unpalatable (to you, that is) friend, you may not have a momentary worry that it is somehow connected with your working, that perhaps it is all your fault. But just compare notes with any non-working mother. That ought to set your mind at ease.

No matter what you do, you are bound to have some guilt if you really do not measure up, whether you work or not. If, for example, you take time off to go to a matinee with a friend instead of attending your daughter's recital, it is reasonable for you to feel guilty. But deep-seated guilt and anxiety that are unconnected with reality are something else again. They are among the most common manifestations of neurosis and stem primarily from unhappy attitudes in childhood. Any detailed discussion of them is outside the scope of this book. If you constantly need reassurance that what you are doing is right, if your guilt is out of all proportion to the true facts of the situation, you would do well to seek professional guidance. In addition to doctors and social workers, many clergymen are skilled in helping you recognize and handle this kind of problem.

### DOMESTIC JOYS

While most mothers who work are glad to relinquish the tedious household chores, many others genuinely regret not having enough time for such household arts as cooking, baking, or sewing. Some consider this part of the price they pay for having an outside job. One mother who started back to work after a few years' absence gave up her Monday night bridge sessions to make enormous batches of brownies (from scratch) for the family. Since everyone loved them and she herself felt that no one else did them quite as well, no one was unhappy with the arrangement.

Another mother found little time for sewing, an activity she very much enjoyed. She substituted crewel embroidery which she could work on easily at meetings or while listening to the children's lessons. She summed up her feelings, and those of many another mother, this way: "I do enjoy most household activities, but I like best the unrepetitive ones I can choose at will. Before I went back to work, when they were imposed as day-to-day routine, I have to admit I chafed under them."

Still another mother reported: "I come home from the office early on Thursdays when Celia, my housekeeper, is off. Then I really go to town preparing the gourmet dinner of the week. My husband and children are always pleased, and I have the best of two worlds. I used to mind a little bit that Celia fed us and knew where everything was, although I knew it was silly— we couldn't get along without her. Now I'm delighted when everyone in the family vies with each other to invite dinner guests for Thursdays."

## ARE YOU REALLY MAKING MONEY?

Many a working mother, totting up the cost of outside services against what she makes, asks herself occasionally: Am I really ahead? Some mothers *do* make money, but others scarcely show any enormous profit. There is, for example the high cost of personal appearance while working, compared with staying-at-home. Clothes that are suitable for working are generally more expensive than at-home togs. A pair of blue jeans and a pullover are many a homemaker's daytime uniform. And a sudsing will do for the jeans, but cleaning bills for business outfits, multiplied by several working days in a week, can add up to a sizable sum.

One mother back at work after a period at home

said she had forgotten "how many pairs of stockings are needed for a working month—and how expensive they are."

Another mother said she loved her work, but her paycheck came pretty close to the salary of the full-time person she hired to care for her house and children. She was somewhat disconcerted when she figured out that even with careful budgeting she earned only a fraction over her helper's salary. But no one minded, least of all her husband, who helped underwrite her days at the office. "Look at it this way, dear," he offered when she expressed some concern over the money she wasn't bringing home, "you said your work was great medicine for you. Think how much cheaper it is than a doctor's bill. And, besides, you're much more interesting to come home to."

It does, of course, cost extra money to run a house and feed a family when you are not always available to track down a bargain or cannot take the time to do-it-yourself.

The most costly item is food. If you shop at a supermarket (and resist impulse buying), it is much less expensive than calling up the grocer who delivers. Most homemakers really like to push carts through racks of beautifully displayed food items, if for no other reason than to keep up with new products. Nearly all markets are open one night during the week, as well as on Saturdays, but your own situation will have to dictate how you spend your time—and your money. And that goes for all kinds of services, too. With or without a good housekeeper, you may decide to send the laundry out or hire a cleaning woman. It all adds up. Only you are in a position to weigh the total cost and decide what is best for you and your family.

Traveling to work may seem a trifle, but even a 15-cent bus ride each way is $1.50 a week and if you take two buses it's $3.00. Near large cities—where the jobs are—commuting from the suburbs is even more expensive. One mother, a social worker who travels a few days a week to New York City from a Westchester suburb said, "It costs me $3.30 just to *move* every day." Here is how she itemized it:

Parking at the Railroad station ................... $ .50
     (the nearer parking lot cost $1 and in
     rain or snow seemed necessary)
Round-trip train fare .................................. 2.50
Bus to the office and back to station ........... .30

Money also goes for lunches, coffee-breaks, newspapers and magazines picked up at the station. It isn't unusual to find a sandwich tucked in the zip compartment of her purse. "Saves me a $2 lunch," she explained, "but it's also great for my waistline."

When you count up the monetary rewards, take into consideration your husband's income tax. He very likely earns more money than you and is consequently in a higher tax bracket. Filing a joint return forces your tax, too, into the higher withholding column. If your husband should happen to be in the 30-50 per cent tax bracket, then the $100 you thought you made this week is really nowhere near that much. This fact may be overlooked until April 15th of the following year.

No one in his right mind (and that now includes the Federal Government) would argue that women should not be paid the same as men for doing the same job. Yet every woman's circle of acquaintances includes at least one friend who makes less per week than a man would make doing identical work.

Most experts today know that women who choose to work do so for a variety of reasons. "True," one psychiatrist said, "many mothers may *say* they work because they need the money, but often this is simply the most socially accepted answer. Some mothers might come out just as well financially by staying home. This doesn't mean they *should* stay home. On the contrary, they very likely realize they are better mothers when they go out to work in spite of the fact that the money they earn doesn't always add up to a sizable sum."

However, in our life today, success is often linked with a pay check. Bringing one home, whether it is added to the family budget, saved for the children's education, immediately paid over to the housekeeper, or used for delicious extras is not nearly as important as what it represents to the individual woman: self-realization.

### EXTRA EFFORT FOR THE EXTRAS

Researchers have found that working mothers spend less time entertaining than do stay-at-home mothers. This is understandable, but if you and your husband like to give parties and don't because of the demands of your job, you might try to streamline your entertainment.

Mrs. McCabe found that Sunday brunches were easy to give. "It's no trouble at all to entertain this way," she told us. "Everyone seems to have a good time, and I'm as relaxed as can be. The only trouble is that it took me too long to make up my mind to have people in on Sundays. If I'd thought of it earlier, I'd have been saved Hank's comments about how my job kept us from entertaining."

Obviously, if you are anti-social, you will not consider a curtailed social life any price to pay for having an outside job. But, if like most people, you enjoy giving and going to occasional parties, you can manage to do both if you make the extra effort.

It takes an extra push, too, to keep on with a hobby or any other special pursuit once you have gone back to work. You may just have to ring down the curtain on TV daytime drama, or learn to live without the late show, but that is hardly a monumental price to pay. For Eleanor King, though, giving up the cello was a genuine sacrifice. She was no great shakes as a musician, but she loved playing with her chamber music group every week. Even though she found her job fascinating and was happy in it, she resented no longer having time for her music.

Her husband came through. He volunteered to take complete charge of the children every Tuesday evening so that she could go off to her group.

"I'm certainly not being put upon," he said. "I really get a kick out of being alone with the kids on Tuesdays. And I'm glad that Eleanor can keep on with her music."

Time alone together, away from children, is hard to come by for most parents, and for those with jobs it appears to be doubly hard. One working mother solved the problem by agreeing to care for her neighbor's children for an entire weekend in exchange for leaving her own youngsters with the neighbors on the following weekend. The plan was such a resounding success that it has become an established custom. Each of the couples feels free to spend an occasional weekend all by themselves. Sometimes they go to a concert or the theater. Or simply to a movie or to visit out-of-town friends. But the point is they allow themselves some time off—to be the man and woman who cared enough about each other to want to spend the rest of their lives together.

## IS THE COST TOO HIGH?

"Don't you miss your children when you're away at work?" a friend asked Jane Kendall. "Yes, of course," answered Jane, "but there are very few times during the year when they themselves are home all day long. Way before I took my part-time job, though, I remember coming home one afternoon after a lunch with friends when Peggy was only about ten months old. I felt just awful when my housekeeper announced that Peggy had stood up and walked across the porch while I was out. I felt *I* should have been the first to see that."

Yet one price every working mother pays is that her helper, and not she, will be on occasion the first to receive some bit of news, remark on some new reaction. As Mrs. Johnson, who works three days a week, said: "I'd like to be home when Jerry, my nine-year-old, comes in from school. Not just because I can remember how I always wanted my mother to be in the house when I came home as a child, but because I like to see him burst in the door, try to imagine what kind of day he's had at school, and get all the news first-hand. However, this moment passes so quickly, and he goes on to something else so soon afterwards, that it would be ridiculous for me to stay home every day for his brief 'Hi,' no matter how much I enjoy it."

Another mother lamented that she had to travel

to town for her job, because "if I were nearby, I could get home sooner and hear the latest teen-age jokes." She laughed, and then added that teen-age jokes, though not always as freshly told, are still in vogue by dinner time and she really could wait till then.

If you work full-time, your day will undeniably be long—longer in some ways than that of the "working father" and fuller certainly of house-home-and-family matters. Even with good help at home, you will be very much in demand after working hours. And in truth you wouldn't want it any other way. You don't count the minutes spent "mothering" with one eye on your children and the other on the clock. Yet to thrive —to remain strong and healthy—that relationship, as you well know, requires proper tending. It takes effort and energy on your part. It means giving freely—love and affection, of course, but also concentrated attention to what might appear on the surface to be minor or even trivial matters. Younger children generally need a larger chunk of your attention and comfort at the day's end but older children require your interest, your help, and guidance in all sorts of situations— school projects and homework, not to mention personal problems and questions that often have to be discussed and solved. Your children want and need to share many of their experiences and adventures with you, and they want you to listen—to *really* listen when they have something to tell you. As every parent knows, it just doesn't do to utter vacant "uh-huh's" while your mind traipses off to a problem of your own.

But, all these must-do's, have-to's, and fun-to-do's take energy and effort, no question about it. Time to be with and do for the youngsters must be distilled into limited, yet nonetheless significant portions. Your endurance and even your patience often have to stretch just a bit further than might be necessary were you at home all day. But most women who have decided they can manage an outside job as well say that it's worth that added ounce (or is it a pound?) of effort. There are minuses, to be sure, but if the pluses far outweigh them, if the satisfactions are greater than the sacrifices, the price you pay is right.

# 10

## BLUEPRINT FOR THE FUTURE

TODAY'S GIRL growing up needs a completely new set of attitudes to grow up by. Why should we continue to send her to school and college to compete with boys in the classroom, to develop an inquiring mind, to show independence and initiative—and then demand that she let only a little bit of all this show once she is married and has children?

"Why don't we do something—and do it fast—to let girls see what their lives are going to be like when they're older?" asks Marilyn Jessup, mother of two. "When I was in college, most of the girls in my class, and that included the brilliant students as well, had only one goal after graduation—finding a good husband. No one ever told them that while marriage and motherhood would no doubt be the most important part of their future, the operative word was *part*."

## EDUCATION FOR WHAT?

A system is certainly outmoded that says a girl may study metaphysics, molecular biology and medieval Latin, share many of the same intellectual interests as the men in her classes, but only until she finds a husband. For as soon as she marries and has a child, she is very often expected to turn her back on her outside activities and find complete fulfillment in caring for her home and family. She is frequently told that her education is primarily something to fall back on—a kind of first-aid kit to keep handy in case she either cannot find a husband or somehow loses him.

"I'm not the only woman I know," a disenchanted homemaker told us, "who woke up at the age of thirty-five to find my kids in school, my housework a cinch, and my life unsatisfying. If I'd been encouraged to keep up with my chemistry which I always loved, I could have managed a course or a lecture now and then while the children were younger. Here I am running to town three days a week to attend graduate classes with young people almost half my age. I'm proud that I can do it, but why didn't I get with it earlier?"

Why *didn't* she get with it earlier? There seems to be almost a conspiracy not to tell the young (though plenty of people are admonishing the middle-aged) that a time will come for them when the role of mother may no longer be enough. And that if they have not all along been working at, say, a part-time job (paid or not), or kept up with their old interests or developed new ones, they are very likely to be involved, not in a teen-age identity crisis, but in a middle-age one of their own.

In an article in *Commonweal*, Katherine Byrne suggests that what may be needed is something to build up the courage of the young and gifted, and keep them in school long enough to stake out a permanent claim in a career worth hanging on to—even by a thread. "Nervous females," she says, "must somehow be assured that all the good men won't be gone if they wait, and that for every girl psychometrician, social anthropologist, or person-with-an-interest-in-Donne there is likely to be a boy who won't hold it against her.

"It would be nice," continues Miss Byrne, "if for each woman who marries and has children, love, generosity, and a free choice among alternatives could be combined in a highly personal mixture, and not according to formulary proscriptions categorically imposed either by the-way-it's-always-been or the latest issue of *McCall's*."

## NATURALLY, WHAT COMES FIRST

For some years now educated women have been offered only one solution. It runs like this: Do meaningful work until you marry. Then for ten years or more concentrate exclusively on your family. After the children need you less than full-time, switch back (if you can) to that rewarding life you knew before. The fallacies, the dangerous implications contained in this sort of advice are all too obvious. No one has pinpointed them more tellingly than Dr. Bruno Bettleheim who wrote: "One result of this sudden switching back and forth in their commitments is that many women resentfully feel that they lived a meaningful life only before they got married—a feeling that can have disastrous effects on them, their marriages, and their children."

Almost as damaging are some currently popular pronouncements which suggest the resurgence of a particularly unattractive form of feminism, mid-20th century style. Strident voices can be heard scolding mothers, urging them out of the house and into a job, preferably a high-powered one. This new prescription for instant fulfillment for one and all is patently absurd. Aside from obvious differences in age and family responsibilities, individual mothers differ markedly—in temperament, taste, and training.

The fact that women *naturally* put marriage and motherhood first seems to have escaped the latter-day feminists who angrily denounce them for not rising up in large numbers to take over the professions, or politics, or the U.N. Many of these critics would have us believe that most of today's women have patterned themselves after a "womanly" image dreamed up by the advertising boys. Others frown on any compromises women make as they attempt to resolve the conflicts involved in the job-motherhood combination. Both camps ignore the fact that most middle-class educated women want to participate actively in the outside world, but not at the expense of their roles as wives and mothers. To imply either that adaptation signifies failure, or that not working for pay means the end of all useful and stimulating endeavor is as false as prescribing demanding jobs as a panacea for one and all.

## HALF A LOAF

"If I could arrange the future," a perceptive mother remarked, "I'd order a climate of opinion that would take for granted that mothers want to do something of value outside the home as well as in. And for those mothers for whom that 'something of value' is a paid job, I'd have the best brains in the country work out new and imaginative ways of using their abilities part-time, especially when the children are young. Not just half-day stints in the local dress or book shop, but acceptance on a part-time basis in jobs we have already trained for—jobs in which we have invested time and energy."

There is ample evidence that such part-time jobs are becoming increasingly available. This is especially so in the case of teachers, social workers, and nurses. Many elementary and high school teachers find a built-in boon in their profession—the substitute teacher program. Although substitutes still are often called on a moment's notice, many mothers report that they have been able to arrange to "sub" on a regular 2- or 3-day week basis, a system easier for them to manage. The pressing need for social workers has led most communities to allow these specialists to arrange their schedules at convenient times. Most hospitals are eager to offer part-time work to qualified nurses.

Other professions and businesses are beginning to welcome the part-time worker. Dental hygienist Dorothy Gilbert found it fairly easy to find a dentist who wanted to hire her only two days a week. Actuary Virginia Leaper was pleased with a letter from her former boss at a small insurance company offering her a job on any part-time basis that would fit into "mutually satisfactory hours." Reporter Jane Summers accepted a job writing news releases every Friday for a fund raising organization.

Still, except where critical shortages exist, not nearly enough has been done to make it easy for the mother who wants a part-time job to find one. "I think employers should take it upon themselves to figure

out ways of helping, and then advertise the results,"
said Margie McMahon, who herself hit on a way to
make her economics training pay off in a three-day-a-
week job in a brokerage house. "One reason they
should want to," she offered, "is that mothers make
good employees." As we have already noted, statistics
do bear out Margie McMahon's thesis. Reports from
employers who hire mothers for part-time work indicate that when women work fewer hours per day or
fewer days per week, their energy, productivity, and
accuracy increase. Absence from work decreases.

A few companies have begun to extend to more
complex jobs the practice started years ago of hiring
students on a work-study program. They hire one person for the morning, another for the afternoon. "Many
different types of really interesting jobs can be handled
in this manner, with two fresh minds half-a-day each,"
a personnel manager said. Unfortunately, most personnel managers cannot find the time to devote to a
study of their company's jobs with this view in mind.
Realizing this, Myra Jacobs, a recent part-time re-
turnee, came up with a suggestion. "Why can't those
employment agencies that specialize in part-time jobs
get busy figuring out a whole horde of jobs that can
be done on a half-day basis? They could turn up a
great many, and once they were seen to work out well,
many women who now say, 'Well, I don't know where
to look' will soon *know* where to look."

## OPPORTUNITIES UNLIMITED

For those who wonder where the jobs are, Jean A. Wells of the Department of Labor's Women's Bureau has this to say: "There is plenty that needs doing and requires the use of all the hands and minds that want to work, if only we can pool and organize our efforts properly. New developments in the fields of atomic energy, satellite communications and electronics are creating more jobs for physical scientists, technicians, engineers, mathematicians, statisticians, and assistants to these various professional workers.

"Continued research and development in medicine and the health services will increase employment opportunities for those in the commonly known health professions and also open up many positions in laboratories, hospitals, and health agencies.

"As nearly everyone is aware, many of the following professions still have shortages: teaching, nursing, school counseling, library work, social work, the social sciences, home economics, dietetics, accountancy, and personnel work. These fields also need many assistant level and subprofessional workers who can perform duties that are somewhat less complicated but nonetheless interesting."

Naturally, many of these jobs will be full-time. Others can be scheduled more flexibly; government, management, and labor, working together, could end the appalling waste of womanpower that now exists.

## NEW ARRANGEMENTS FOR JUNIOR

Today the chief child-care arrangement for the middle-class mother who works is hired help. Much could be done for the future if more thought and energy were directed toward the problem of getting *qualified* household assistance—and if society were convinced of the wisdom of doing so. More agencies, both private and governmental, that specialize in seeking out and training potential helpers can be established. Upgrading the status and the pay of child-care jobs is an obvious necessity. If refresher courses were offered to the large numbers of older women who have already raised their own families and who want *their* outside jobs to be caring for children, we would reasonably expect to find many eager recruits. Training can also be provided to many others, including those formerly in jobs now mechanized. The Manpower Development and Training Act, passed primarily to help unemployed workers learn new skills, and the Vocational Educational Act of 1963 are two measures which might conceivably be used to remedy the present situation.

Another solution to the problem of who-will-help-care-for-Junior is the establishment of professionally run centers. Only in the United States is it considered subversive to entrust the care of young children for a few hours a day or a week to competent, well-trained specialists, unless, of course, mother is on the relief rolls. Both working and non-working middle-class mothers (as well as their children) could benefit from such services, as has been amply demonstrated in many other parts of the world. And certainly much more imaginative use could be made of the public schools for the after-hour activities of youngsters.

To those die-hard critics of anything less than "full-time mothering," another reminder is in order. There is no evidence to show that stay-at-home mothers have produced children who are any better off or more adequately prepared for adulthood than others.

### CULTURAL LAG: THE BUGABOO

One hopeful sign that needed changes may be in the cards is the arrival on the scene of a vast new group of pacesetters—those educated, energetic, interested young mothers, freed from the once time-consuming chores of housework, who are determined to be participating members of society. Spurred by them, society is beginning to alter the traditional image of motherhood.

One new-look mother, Mimi Nelson, with two youngsters in school, and a master's degree in psychology (accomplished after marriage) has many ideas for a more ideal climate for working mothers. "We could use many agencies to provide working mothers with lots of services to make life easier for them," says Mimi. "The need is clear, but that old bugaboo, cultural lag, binds us by our own apron strings."

Cultural lags are never closed overnight. In fact, barring a major upheaval such as a world-wide depression or full-scale war, social change usually straggles far to the rear of actual need for it. Mimi is convinced that no such emergency will be needed to shake into being a new look for the world of working mothers.

Today the middle-income group comprises a majority of our population. Mothers who are pleased to describe themselves as belonging to "the great middle class" have become a dictating influence. They are, in general, the ones who are free to choose whether to work solely within the family or to assume additional outside responsibilities. As more and more of these mothers decide to work outside the home, we are bound to see a change in the attitudes of society and in the provisions it offers to make a full life a reality for more women. Many Mimi Nelsons are now arguing for up-to-date provisions for the care of their house, help in handling the free time of their children, flexible scheduling of working hours, and a realization by society that the old stereotypes are no longer valid. It is to be hoped that many communities will follow the lead suggested in the report of the President's Commission on the Status of Women and offer more services to *many* types of families so that any woman who wants to take an outside job can do so without an excessive burden of either work or guilt.

## SMALLER FAMILIES BACK IN STYLE

"If it's possible to judge by my daughter-in-law and most of her friends, it seems to me that smaller families are coming back in style," remarked one working grandmother. She may be right, for there are signs that the birth rate is beginning to decline and that families will indeed be smaller in the years ahead. A college professor reports that he has been asking his students over the past several years how many children they wanted. "As might be expected," he disclosed, "they overwhelmingly want two, three, or four. But the interesting fact is that more now want two than four. Compared with the 1940's and 1950's, this is a significant change."

Not only is it a significant change, it is long over-due. Aside from the realization that unlimited pro-creation is a grave world danger, tomorrow's daughters will hopefully come to view motherhood and child-rearing as the valuable and satisfying aspects of their lives they truly are, but not as the sole basis for achieving feelings of worth and self-realization.

"I'm fairly certain my girls aren't going to become the fertility champions many of my college classmates turned into," said one bright mother of two bright daughters. "Judy, my oldest, and her husband consider the outsize family a luxury from many standpoints, financial, intellectual, and human. And while young Ellen and her fiancé, both of whom are now in law school, look forward to having a family some day, they are convinced that too many parents of large broods are signing I.O.U.'s that their children will eventually have to pay off in terms of crowding and congestion, schooling at all levels that is bound to be inferior, and a style of living stripped of much that is graceful and agreeable."

As more and more women build fuller lives for themselves, there is every reason to believe that the baby marathon will be called off, viewed no longer as a status symbol or an existence justifier. And we'll all be better off as a result. Quality, after all, not quantity, is what the world really needs today.

### MORE ALIKE THAN DIFFERENT

"In my blueprint for the future," says architect-mother Barbara Vincent, "I'd like to see society make an about-face in its thinking about men's and women's roles. Take my sister and brother-in-law, for example. No matter what the day's been like, he can't bring himself to lend her a hand after dinner, and if she asks him to take care of the children while she gets her hair done, he considers it a personal affront. I'd like to see all of us reach the point where mother can change a washer in the faucet as easily and well as father can change a damp toddler, with nobody judging their femininity or masculinity by such superficialities. Frank and I aren't like my sister and her family, thank goodness. Our children never think of Daddy as not being a man because he gives them their bath, or me as unwomanly because I have a job I like."

As Barbara Vincent suggests, a wholesale reform of attitudes is overdue. Perhaps it is not too much to hope that in the future our society will be able to acknowledge how very much men and women are alike, while appreciating, of course, the ways in which they are truly different. Such a society will not need to label as unfeminine or neurotic the needs of many modern mothers to be seriously involved in work beyond the confines of their own homes, nor to stifle their ambitions with what Mary I. Bunting, President of Radcliffe, calls the "hidden persuader that tells a woman it is unladylike to use her mind."

With greater understanding of what a modern and satisfying life can be for people of both sexes, women will be encouraged to develop and continue their serious interests, and men helped to become certain enough of their own masculinity that they need not fear their wives' desires for self-realization.

Obviously, this will not happen overnight, but it can come about. We all have the responsibility to re-examine our own attitudes critically and to use courage and imagination in planning intelligently for the future. Complacency never moves a culture forward.

## THE FINAL GOAL

As has been amply documented, full-time motherhood is in truth a myth. Living only for one's children can be a very real danger, hindering, as it almost always does, the sound development of the young. Even if it were possible to fill all one's time and devote all one's energies to the undeniably important task of creating a happy home and rearing healthy offspring, children do eventually grow up and move away. Young, middle-aged, or old, all discontented mothers are either injustice collectors or injustice distributors, or combinations of both. Fifty years ago, Thorstein Veblen wrote: "Woman is endowed with her share—which there is reason to believe is more than an even share—of the instinct of workmanship, to which futility of life or of expenditure is obnoxious." When women feel unhappy and aggrieved at not being fully used, it is not only their own plight that evokes concern, but also that of their husbands and children who cannot help being affected in turn.

Any blueprint for the future will encourage all

women to find their own paths—either through jobs or in other satisfying ways—to richer, more rewarding lives. Then women can view marriage and motherhood as a significant part of life—but not the whole of it— and certainly not a part that causes them to throw away in anger or boredom or submission their talents and their capabilities.